MUSIC AT COURT

1. *Musicians at a Florentine wedding (mid–fifteenth century).*

MUSIC AT COURT

Christopher Hogwood

LONDON
THE FOLIO SOCIETY
1977

PRINTED IN GREAT BRITAIN
Printed and bound by T & A Constable Ltd, Edinburgh
Set in 12 point Linotron Bembo spaced 1 point

CONTENTS

2. *Water music c.1520; a musical party of nobles, with flute, lute and singers.*

INTRADA

'Never criticize the composition of a Royal Highness. You never know who may have written it.' The recommendation is by Brahms, but it could as easily have come from Dufay or Couperin, from Mozart or Machaut; the cynicism reflects a long tradition of tactful silence on the part of courtiers faced with the courtly assumption of culture by their princes. Henry VIII did not hesitate to add an extra line of counterpoint to a perfectly complete Flemish *chanson*, together with his signature at the end of the work, and modern musicology, scorning Brahms's advice, has returned the work to its rightful source. But who would feel that the reputation of Hayne van Ghizeghem has been diminished by the theft? On the contrary, the king's name, then as now, has assured if not immortality, at least a popular notoriety which has served the music well. More relevant is the fact that a monarch was expected to compose, and was trained to do so. If an academic eyebrow is raised at the king's ingenuous system of composing, it may relax before the irrefutable evidence of his prowess as a performer, and the enormous collections of musical instruments with which he filled his palaces. Nor can Henry be considered unique in his musical gifts. His daughter Mary was 'singularly accomplished, most particularly in music, playing on every instrument, especially on the lute and *arpichordo*', Elizabeth's proficiency is famous, and Charles I could 'play his part exactly well on the Bass-Viol'. Add to this English ensemble George I on the viola, 'poor Fred', Prince of Wales on the cello, and George III on the violin; the light tenor of

3. *Frederick Prince of Wales, accompanied by his sisters on the harpsichord and English guitar; Kew House in the background (Philip Mercier, 1733).*

Albert, Prince Consort, would need a little foreign help, perhaps from the four Hapsburg princesses who acquitted themselves so well in an opera specially written for them by Hasse, before a comparable vocal group could be presented. Even so it is doubtful whether this band could offer very strong competition to Frederick the Great on the flute, Count Razoumowsky on the cello and the Hapsburg profile of Archduke Rudolf at the piano: they would, naturally, all play their own compositions.

Such talented amateurs were classified as *dilettanti* prior to the twentieth century — a title that carried no overtones of superficiality, nor any hint of ambition. It was the *professori* who pursued the art for a living. Henry Peacham recommended in his *Compleat Gentleman* of 1627 that music be cultivated in moderation, and not to such an extent that a man neglect his more weighty employments; Castiglione's *Courtier* played when he was 'in familiar, and loving company, having nothing elles a doe'.

A practical training in music, even if not displayed in public, was considered necessary for princes in their role as patrons. Patronage was an aspect of power, and a ruler needed to be capable of distinguishing the good from the bad without ministerial advice. Even the least musical of monarchs admitted the necessity of being seen to encourage the arts; architecture was the most permanent form of self-recommendation, painting the most flattering, but there was no more stirring combination of sound and spectacle than music. Renaissance princes were not slow to realize that the ancient world was remembered for its arts rather than its institutions, and they satisfied their hunger for immortality by continual patronage. Stuart monarchs found the most persuasive vehicle for political propaganda in the elaborations of the court masque, and the Sun King marked each of his European military successes with an opera that ostensibly applauded the victories of the classical world. The disguise was thin but necessary: it was, after all, more decorous to be described as Jupiter in recitative than in cold print.

   Music was political propaganda, a display of power and wealth, a sphere for competition with rival courts and a palliative for those who were less than enchanted with affairs at home. 'Persons of high degree who patronize music,' said Kuhnau, 'do so for reasons of state, in order to distract the people and prevent them from looking into their cards.' But these were no principles to

4. *An open-air performance of Lully's* Alceste *at Versailles in 1674. The orchestra is divided to allow the king an uninterrupted view of the stage.*

attract Monteverdi, Bach or Haydn. If the motives of patronage could be interpreted in so Machiavellian a spirit, what induced the greatest performers and composers to seek service in such courts?

Money, of course, features prominently. In an uncertain Europe racked with inter-state wars, with legislation against 'vagabonds' which was taken to apply to unattached musicians, with no copyright protection for a composer's own music, the security of a court salary was the only sanctuary outside the Church. Money was lavished on all forms of music, but particularly on opera, 'the spectacle of princes' as Gagliano called it. The Duke of Brunswick went so far as to sell his own subjects as soldiers in order to finance the excesses of his court opera, while Charles Eugene of Württemberg, finding no such expedient, bankrupted his whole state.

Opera was one of several composite art-forms that flourished as a result of court patronage; the masque, the *ballet de cour*, the 'magnificences' of the Valois rulers, all required an alliance of talents difficult to achieve outside a court setting. Such corporate ventures offered a continuity of experience as sustaining to art as was continuity of breeding in the families that promoted them, and the artist

5. *Court musicians at Florence. The violinist is holding an out-curved bow typical of the early eighteenth century.*

6. *A design for a triumphal arch by a member of the Bibiena family. On either side of the square is an ornamental platform, each with an orchestra (c. 1700).*

found a further advantage in the transfusion of foreign talent that gave added lustre to the spectacles. Italians were the most frequent (and best paid) foreigners: Catherine de' Medici brought her household players with her to the Valois court (together with her cooks, and a delicacy hitherto unknown in France — ice-cream); James I paid his Italian players double the salary offered to his English employees, and in the eighteenth century Italian castrati and violinists ruled throughout Europe. 'Wee cannot wonder,' wrote Roger North in his individual orthography, 'that among the courters of musick an Itallian taste should prevaile.' One major reason was the arrival of Corelli's music in England — 'the onely musick relished for a long time. Add to this, that most of the yong nobility and gentry that have travelled into Italy affected to learne of Corelli, and brought home with them such favour for the Itallian musick, as has given it possession of our pernassus. And the best utensill of Apollo, the violin, is so universally courted, and sought after to be had of the best sort, that some say England hath dispeopled Italy of violins.'

Travelling, with its concomitant exposure to fashion, had never been difficult for musicians — the itinerant troubadour and the independent minstrel were the earliest of the temporary employees supported by a court. But travel with access to the leaders of taste, with security and a safe-conduct, was a luxury that only the dispensation of a nobleman could assure — even as late as 1775 Charles Burney thanked the Earl of Sandwich for the introductions and patronage that had made feasible his tours round Europe. For economy, as well as camouflage, it was not unknown for musicians to combine their art with espionage abroad. A ready payment from the Secret Service funds of James I was waiting for John Dowland on his return from employment in the court of Denmark; and in the eighteenth century there was the 'famous Count St Germaine, who made so much noise at that time, not only with his fiddle, but his mysterious conduct and equivocal character. This prince,' Burney added, 'is now retired from the world.'

In 1664 young Pelham Humfrey, the most talented of Captain Cooke's boys in the Chapel Royal, was sent to France by Charles II to absorb the style and technique of Lully and the twenty-four violins. Payment in the same year from the Secret Service fund, 'to defray the charge of his journey into France and Italy, £200', was an implausibly large amount! According to Pepys he was not improved by his travels:

. . . calling at my mercer's and tailor's, and there I find, as I expected, Mr Caeser and little Pelham Humphreys, lately returned from France, and is an absolute monsieur, as full of form, and confidence, and vanity, and disparages everything, and everybody's skill but his own. The truth is, everybody says he is very able, but to hear how he laughs at all the King's Music here, as Blagrave and others, that they cannot keep time not tune, nor understand anything; and that Grebus, the Frenchman, the King's master of the Music, how he understands nothing, nor can play on any instrument, and so cannot compose: and that he will give him a lift out of his place; and that he and the King are mighty great! and that he hath already spoke to the King of Grebus would make a man piss.

Despite Humfrey's arrogant manner, his reaction to foreign stimulus was exactly what a good patron anticipated. The rivalry and competition that it encouraged supplied an antidote to the comfort and security offered at court, which could all too easily lead to extravagance, monopoly and complacency. The incentive to excel, particularly against foreign opposition, excited talented composers like Humfrey, who in his turn provided a lead followed by the younger Henry Purcell — the greatest of England's court protegés, who never

7. *Violin, lute and bass-viol players included in the courtyard of a Venetian palace (c. 1620).*

left the boundaries of London. Such was the continuity of court patronage, and the transmission of experience that it could provide.

A composer's obligations to his patron were often spelled out in detail. Haydn's contract with Prince Paul Anton Esterházy was thought to be rather up-to-date for the 1760s, although we may find it excessively feudal in its demands.★ Even beyond the categories of obedience set down in print, there were relationships that sometimes restrained the more emancipated artist of the nineteenth century. Music commissioned by his patron, Haydn learned, had to be tailored to match his technique; anything too difficult was returned curtly, for rewriting. On the other hand, he could not indulge a tactless delight in his own virtuosity; 'It is no credit to you that you play better than I do,' the prince ungraciously explained, 'it is your duty.' Similar obligations still held good when the individual voice of the musician had been heard in post-Revolution Europe. Count Razoumovsky could still expect, and receive, a cello part of particular importance in the quartets he commissioned from Beethoven, despite the growing philosophy that art should be expected to bite the hand that fed it.

★ See page 103.

8. *'The Triumph of Isabella.' The second car in the procession that took place in Brussels on 31 May 1615 contains Isabella, daughter of the Hapsburg Archduke Albert, and the fourth car represents Apollo and the Muses.*

The young Weber, employed at the age of twenty by Duke Eugene of Württemberg, took great care to include a prominent oboe part in his first symphony, knowing that the duke was himself a keen amateur oboist.

In every era the uneasy partnership between the artist and society has always involved some sacrifice, either of career or conscience. On the highest level of collaboration the artist can accept whole-heartedly the ideas and ideals of the society that supports him, and at the same time achieve a significance of style in his creations that rises above the local experience which generated them. The expert patron knows when not to criticize; Lorenzo de' Medici, springing to the defence of one of his organists, admonished one critic: 'If only you knew how difficult it is to attain perfection in any art.' The prudent ruler remembers the advice a courtier is said to have given to Louis IV: 'Know, Sire, that a king without any taste for music is a crowned ass.' Whether moved by prudence or expertise, the courts of Europe present a panorama of enlightened patronage unrivalled by any other institution of the past, and unmatched by any council, corporation or committee of the present.

I

PRINCES OF HEAVEN AND EARTH

'When I see the winter returning, then I must find me a lodging. O that I might discover a generous host who would make no charge, but would offer me pork and beef and mutton, ducks, pheasants and venison, fat hens and capons and . . . good cheeses in baskets.'

The plight of Colin Muset, the thirteenth century trouvère, alone, homeless, and with the chill nights drawing in, has been repeated in many later centuries; but in medieval and renaissance Europe relief could be expected from only two sources — the church and the court. Life with a prince was certainly the more adventurous choice. Richard Coeur-de-Lion is reputed to have been discovered in captivity only by the efforts of his fellow trouvère, Blondel, who wandered Europe singing outside every prison and castle, until eventually his song was answered by Richard from within the castle of Dürenstein in Austria. Legend or not, a ballad that Richard himself composed in captivity has survived; an eloquent and, considering his position, restrained text set to one of the most evocative of trouvère melodies.

> *Ja nus hons pris ne dira sa raison*
> *adroitement, se dolantement non;*
> *mes par confort puet il fere chançon.*
> *moult ai amis, mes povre sont li don;*
> *honte en avront, se por ma reançon*
> *sui ces deus yvers pris.*

Ce sevent bien my honme et mi baron,
Englois, Normant, Poitevin et Gascon,
que je n'avoie se povre conpaignon,
cui je laissasses por avoir en prixon.
je nel di pas por nule retraçon,
mas encor sui ge pris.

No prisoner will ever state his case cleverly,
he will put it in a sorrowful way;
he can, however, write a poem to comfort himself.
I have many friends but their gifts are few in number.
They will be shamed if I remain in captivity these two winters
if my ransom is not paid.

My men and barons,
from England, Normandy, Poiton and Gascony,
know that if I had a friend,
I would not leave him in prison, however humble he was,
if it was just a question of money.
I don't say this as a reproach,
but I am still held a prisoner.

'A verse without music is a mill without water,' explained one of the troubadours, and this interdependence of words and music typifies the greatest products of the Age of Courtly Love. Guillaume de Machaut was a fine example of the synthesis of talent that the medieval court could discover. In addition to

9. *A fifteenth-century miniature showing the two Burgundian composers Guillaume Dufay (with a portative organ) and Gilles Binchois (with a 'Gothic' harp).*

being in holy orders, and writing the words to almost all his own music, he was also secretary to John of Luxembourg, that greatest of European knights, who eventually became King of Bohemia. The chivalry of knights recorded in verse was not so far from real life as it might seem today; Machaut's master even went to his death at the battle of Crécy in demonstration of this ideal. Old, blind and failing in health, he nevertheless rode out with the greatest warriors of France on that fateful day; to us it might seem futile, but to his contemporaries it was the epitome of a chivalrous death.

   The conventions of courtly love convey to us a similar sense of unreality. Unrequited love and the misery of the petitioner may have been literary and musical conventions, but in the hands of men like Machaut, the subtle blend of music and poetry might have melted the heart of the cruellest mistress. One of the best reflections of this etiquette is Mauchaut's autobiographical *Le Livre du*

16.   *Three shawms contribute to a marriage feast at the court of King Yon of Gascony.*

11. *Love songs copied into a heart-shaped manuscript for Jean de Montchenu, brother of the Duc de Savoie (c. 1470).*

voir-dit, telling of his extended love affair (although he was over sixty and blind in one eye) with the young Péronne

> I have no wish to see how handsome Absalom is,
> Nor how wise and eloquent Ulysses,
> Nor to learn of Samson's strength
> and see Delilah shear his locks.
>
> I care not one whit for Argus's eyes,
> nor nay greater joy.
> My pleasure is a simple one.
> for the sight of my lady fulfils all my desires.

Sadly Péronne was not seriously interested in the aging poet and musician, although Mauchaut's own story tells of them living happily ever after. This conventionality of *Amour Courtois* is upheld by the charming illumination, depicting the happy couple in bed, while Venus blows a convenient cloud across the picture to ward off prying eyes.

Sensibility, Rhetoric and Music, the three children of Nature that met in

Machaut's philosophy, were to attain even greater prominence as the court of Burgundy flourished and the fortunes of the French monarchy declined. Agincourt was the turning point, and although the celebration of the English victory was expressed straightforwardly enough in the *Agincourt Carol*, the aspirations and rituals of the Burgundian Court took a more complicated form. There is almost no other period of history when the interweaving of the arts in the context of royal patronage was so lovingly and meticulously described as by the chroniclers of Philip the Good, Charles the Bold, and other monarchs with such useful epithets as 'the Fair' or 'the Rash'. The paintings of Memling and Van Eyck preserve in detail the proliferation of musical instruments that delighted the poets and patrons of that time. On the death of Philip the Good, the whole assembly of music was called on to lament 'the illustrious Duke of Burgundy':

> Pipes, drums, timpani and trumpets,
> Lutes, portatives, harps, psalteries,
> Drums, bassets, bells and sonnets,
> Horns, bagpipes, sweet symphonies,
> Chansons on the clavichord,
> Proportions, sweet prolations,
> Perfections of long and breves,
> Blend your sounds in the dissonances of grief . . .

From the poetry, paintings, tapestries and stained glass of this period we learn of the enormous variety of instruments available to the court composer, though less about the way the music itself was performed.

The enthusiasm of the Court of Burgundy for variety and vividness was apparent in the visual arts. Skill at combining the old principles of chivalry with visual and musical effects was displayed in the pageantry, processions, feastings and joustings that gave ample demonstration of their wealth and of the proficiency of the *ménestrels*, those skilled musicians who were, primarily, entertainers.

Rivalry with the court of France, of course, spurred on Philip the Good, but chivalry also played a part — at least, in intention. When Philip married his third wife, Isabella of Portugal in 1430, she was greeted at her entrance into the city by 'at least 120 silver trumpets' and the singers at the ceremony were 'the very best in the art of music one could possibly find anywhere'. To mark the marriage, Philip created a new order of chivalry, the Order of the Golden Fleece. In 1454, with the intention of rallying the Burgundian nobles around his banner to mount yet another Crusade, he invited the Chevaliers of the order to the Banquet of the Oath of the Pheasant. Each knight was to vow to crusade against the Turks and relieve the mother church of Constantinople, which had fallen the previous year. These chivalrous intentions came to nothing, but the descriptions of the feast itself, which we have from two avowedly eye-witness accounts, present a picture of pomp and ceremony in which music played no small part. The *Mémoires* of Olivier de la Marche, the organizer of the scenic effects and in his own account the star of the show, give the most elaborate description of the setting.

The hall in which the feast was held was large and the walls covered with a tapestry depicting scenes from the life of Hercules. To enter this hall there were five doors, each guarded by archers in uniforms of grey and black. . . . Inside there were three tables laid out, one of medium size, one large and one small. On the medium one there was a church, with windows, very properly made, and a bell that rang and inside four singers who sang and played on an organ when their turn came. . . . There was also another decoration consisting of a small child naked on a rock pissing rose-water continuously. . . . On the second table there was a huge pie, in which there were twenty-eight living people playing on

12. Chasse au faucon à la cour de Philippe le Bon. *A typical Burgundian basse-danse ensemble consisted of two shawms and slide-trumpet.*

13. *Angels playing psaltery, tromba marina, lute, slide-trumpet and shawm (Hans Memling).*

divers instruments, each when their turn came. [Was this the origin, one wonders, of the 'four-and-twenty blackbirds' in the nursery rhyme pie?] The second edifice on this table was a castle, on the highest tower of which was Melusine in the form of a serpent, while from two other towers orange water would cascade into the moat whenever one wished . . . also a windmill, a scene of a desert with a tiger, marvellously lifelike, which fought with a serpent, and a savage seated on a camel . . . while on the third table, which was smaller than the others there was a marvellous forest, just like a forest in India, and in this forest several strange-looking beasts which moved by themselves just as though they were alive. When everyone was in position and the guests were seated, the bell of the church, which was on the first table, suddenly rang loudly; when it stopped, three trebles and a tenor sang a very sweet *chanson*; what it was I cannot tell for sure, but it seemed to me to be a pleasing grace for the beginning of the meal. When they had finished a shepherd from the pie played on the bagpipe in a very novel fashion. Immediately he had finished, through the doorway of the hall

14. *Angels playing two slide-trumpets, portative organ, 'Gothic' harp and medieval fiddle (Hans Memling).*

came a horse, wearing a coat of orange silk, and bearing two trumpeters seated back to back, who sounded a fanfare on their trumpets. . . . When the horse tableau had passed, the organ in the church began to play very softly, and in the pie a German cornett played in a very strange way . . . next a *chanson* from the church, and a *doucaine* with another instrument accompanying it from the pie, and suddenly a very cheerful fanfare from four trumpets. These trumpets were behind a green curtain, hung over a great scaffolding built at the end of the hall. When the fanfare was ended, the curtain was suddenly drawn, and there was seen the personage of Jason, in full armour, walking about and looking round as though he had just arrived in a foreign land. . . . After his battle with a dragon, the organ in the church played a piece about as long as a motet, two blind musicians in the pie played on hurdy-gurdys and then three sweet voices sang a *chanson* called '*Sauvegarde de ma vie*'. Then through the door, after those in the church and those in the pastry had each performed four times, there entered into the hall a wondrously great and beautiful stag: upon the stag was mounted a young lad, about twelve years old. The child held the two horns of the stag with his two hands. When he entered into the hall, he began the upper part of a *chanson*, very high and clear: and the stag sang the tenor, without there being any other person except the child and the artifice of the said stag; and the song that they sang was named '*Je ne vis oncques la pareille*'. While singing, as I have narrated to you, they made the rounds before the table, and then returned; and this interlude seemed to me good. After this interlude of the white stag and the child, the singers sang a motet in the church, and in the pastry a lute was played with two good voices, and the church and the pastry always did something between the interludes.

But the *pièce de résistance* was yet to come:

Through the same door that all the other characters had come suddenly appeared a giant, dressed in a long silk robe, and leading an elephant, also in silk, with a castle on its back, and in this castle was a lady, in white satin in the style of a nun, but wearing a black mantle over it. As all the company was wondering who this lady could be, her elephant stopped and she began her lament.

It transpires that the lady (who was actually played by Olivier de la Marche himself) represented the Mother Church at the mercy of the Infidel (the elephant), and the lament she sang (in falsetto) was designed to move the hearts of the assembled company before they took their vows.

Perhaps it was the calming influence of hindsight (since he did not write his memoirs until almost half a century after these events took place) that led Olivier de la Marche to conclude, somewhat unconvincingly: 'to cut a long story short, the banquet was over, the tables were cleared, everyone left the hall, and I thought it must all have been a dream, since all that remained to be seen was a fountain. Yet I reflected on the outrageous excesses and the vast expense of such feasts, which occur very infrequently.'

One wonders just how long this entertainment took!

Though every other aspect of the feast is described in great detail, no mention is made of the composers of the music. This is particularly strange since '*Je ne vis oncques la pareille*' (a very apt title in this context) is attributed to Binchois, while the final *Lamentatio* is almost certainly one of those that Dufay mentions writing during that year. Probably both composers, the two greatest *chanson* writers of their generation, were present at the feast, although neither was attached to the duke's musical establishment.

As well as giving the modern performer a marvellously vivid picture of the way various types of instruments could be used and combined, the accounts of this lavish entertainment emphasize the fact that the nobility did not perform on such occasions. Music was appreciated, spectacles were applauded, but there was no involvement, other than by the narrator of the story.

Exactly the same detachment can be seen in the musical enterprises of the Emperor Maximilian, who knew the ways of the Burgundian court at first hand from his marriage with Mary of Burgundy. No doubt his gastronomic as well as his musical tastes were influenced by the finesse of the most elegant court in Europe. From Austria he wrote: 'We are sending you herewith a young fellow called Josse Weert, who has served in our kitchen, and we wish him to learn to make *pâtés* in the Low Country manner, asking you to place him with your master baker . . . you will do us a great favour.'

On the musical front he set about establishing his Hofkapelle, a collection of musicians rivalling any in Europe. Music he saw as a strong weapon in the

15. *'How the young Weisskunig learned to know music and stringed instruments'*
(Woodcut by Hans Burgkmair).

campaign of pageantry and propaganda which he had to wage throughout his vast empire; the Hapsburg profile needed every assistance to ingratiate itself with the princes of Christendom.

Elaborate publications marked the stages by which he transmitted his approved biography to the world; partly fictional, wholly propaganda, they presented the components of his musical household, and, in an idealized form, his own initiation into music. The *Weisskunig* sequence of woodcuts is a sad token of an emperor who could believe that he would only be remembered according to the amount of money he spent on his own glorification during his lifetime. In the scene that depicts 'How the young Weisskunig learned to know music and stringed instruments' we find him assuming a deified posture, making no contact with any of the various players around him. But the ensemble, naturally enough, is comprehensive, in the background are four singers and a cornet player (blowing the instrument, as so many early pictures show, from the *side* of his mouth). All varieties of chordal instruments are to be found: the organ and the virginals (or might it be a clavichord?), with harp in the foreground, and the lute still in its case. Wind instruments include a flute, a crumhorn and a set of

16. *Philip the Good, Duke of Burgundy, dressed in the Order of the Golden Fleece.*

17. *The unmistakable Hapsburg profile: Maximilian I, his wife,*
Mary of Burgundy, and their family.

recorders, while the group in the foreground consists of those instruments most suggestive of military campaigning: drums, a *tromba marina* and a sackbut.

Of all these categories, the one which has proved the most lasting is, ironically, the most remote in the illustration. The Hofmusik-kapelle which Maximilian founded on 7 July 1498 still exists today, and provides the music for services in the Hofburg in Vienna. Countless generations of gifted boys have been trained as *Singknaben*, and the Vienna Boys Choir, as the establishment is known in English, is the outcome of Maximilian's patronage.

The emperor was so insistent that his glory should not be obliterated by time that he devised what he hoped would be a permanent record of his retinue in a series of extravagant woodcuts, made by Burgkmair, Dürer and other leading artists. Again there is no sign of Maximilian taking any active part — the nearest he approaches to creativity is a tentative credit as the author of the words of '*Innsbruck ich muss dich lassen*'. *The Triumph* presents an impressive inventory of the musical resources of the Imperial court. All the musicians and their instruments appear in groups in the various triumphal chariots, with the exception of the organist Paul Hofhaimer, the most versatile of the imperial musicians, who has a chariot to himself. He frequently travelled with the emperor on campaigns, and it is hardly surprising to read that his instruments weighing '*80 livres et plus*' were only transported '*avec grand paine, travail et fatigue de corps*'.

In contrast to this impersonal deployment of musical troops, we have only to turn to Maximilian's younger contemporary in England ('our vindictive and voluptuous monarch' in Burney's phrase), to find a much greater personal involvement in the performance of music. Henry VIII, on a progress in 1510 was 'exercisyng hym self daily in shotyng, singing, dancyng, wrastelyng, casting of the barre, plaiying at the recorders, flute, virginals, and in setting of songes, makyng of balettes, and dyd set ii goodly masses, every of them fyve partes'. Quite how all these activities were fitted in *daily* is hard to imagine, unless some could be pursued simultaneously, though there is no doubting either the king's musical competence or his lust for life.

> Pastime with good company
> I love and shall until I die
> Grudge who lust, but none deny,
> So God be pleased this life will I
> > For my pastance,
> > Hunt, sing, and dance,
> > My heart is set,
> > All goodly sport
> > To my comfort
> > Who shall me let?
> Youth will needs have dalliance,
> Of good or ill some pastance;
> Company me thinketh best
> All thought and fancies to digest,
> > For idleness
> > Is chief mistress
> > Of vices all;
> > Then who can say
> > But mirth and play
> > Is best of all?

18. *The musicians' gallery at Whitehall by Holbein.*

Company with honesty
Is virtue — and vice to flee;
Company is good or ill
But every man hath his free will.
   The best I sue,
   The worst eschew;
   My mind shall be
   Virtue to use;
   Vice to refuse
   I shall use me.

Following the example of Richard I, Henry was responsible for both music and words in that declaration of youthful principles. The same cannot be said, however, for several other compositions that bear his name; the ominously titled four-part setting of '*Hélas Madame*' turns out to be a well-known Flemish *chanson* in three-parts, to which the king added a poor inner part and his own signature. (Brahms might well have felt vindicated in his warning!)

In Henry's reign the many minstrels who had found a comfortable place at the court of his predecessors found their services no longer needed. A new organization, The Kinge's Musicke, consisting of both singers and instrumentalists, had been selected to travel with him and supply entertainment. Eight viols, seven sackbuts, seven flutes, two lutes, thirteen singers, a virginalist, a bagpiper, a rebec player and, sensibly enough, two instrument repairers appear on the lists. Their names show that Henry spurned local talent: Hans Hosent, Fraunces de Venice, Ambrose de Milano, Philip van Welder and many more exotic were his chosen entertainers. Of the Italians whom Henry attracted to his court, the most favoured was the Venetian monk, Dionisio Memmo who arrived in 1516 and immediately charmed the king by his playing on an organ he had brought over specially 'at great expense'. With his usual disregard for religious scruple, Henry immediately wrote to Rome asking to have the friar defrocked and within months he was installed in Henry's retinue. 'After dinner, His Majesty took the ambassador into the Queen's chamber, giving him amusements of every description, the chief of which was the instrumental music of the reverend Dionisio Memmo, his chaplain, which lasted four consecutive hours.' By contrast, the Spanish ambassador reports, indigenous playing was less efficient: two English organists played a duet (the earliest duet to be mentioned), but 'very ill forsooth; they kept bad time, and their touch was feeble, neither was their execution good'. Not every foreigner could please: Memmo's success prompted Zuan de Leze, an illegitimate son of the Lord Lieutenant of Cyprus, to try for a position in England as a harpsichordist. But when his performance did not meet with Henry's approval, the disappointed candidate went away and hanged himself.

Amongst all the king's musical pursuits the keyboard seems to have been preferred. The careful inventories of his enormous instrument collection indicate that a keyboard instrument was required in every one of his establishments, and often in every room, along with an impressive assortment of other instruments.

Stuffe and Implements at GRENEWICHE.

In the Kynges priuey Chambre.

One paier of Regalles with the case.

AT WESTMINSTER.

Item. A paire of double Regalles of latten with iii Stoppes of pipes couered with purple vellat enbrawdered all over with damaske pirles and Venice golde and the Cover thereof the inner parte covered with crimeson vellat likewise enbrawdered with damaske pirles havinge a stele Glasse in the same and the Kinges Armes and Quene Janes Armes likewise enbrawdered with a cover the pipes couered with crimeson vellat likewise enbrawdered havinge a rose crowned upon the same

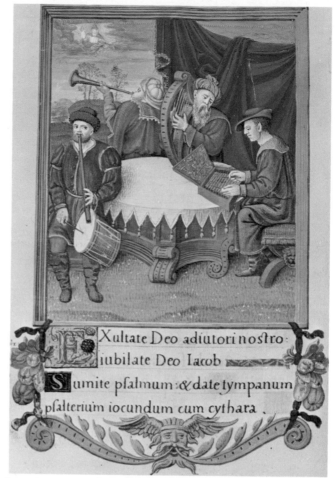

19. *The instruments of Psalm 81 illustrated in Henry VII's psalter. The psaltery and the dulcimer were basically the same instrument, the one plucked and the other played with small sticks, as here.*

Xultate Deo adiutori nostro:
iubilate Deo Iacob
Sumite psalmum :& date tympanum
psalterium iocundum cum cythara

standinge uppon a foote of wainscott painted in Rabeske woorke wherein liethe the Bellowes.

Item. An Instrumente with a double Virgynall and a double Regall with iii Stoppes of pipes, of woode painted with grene Rabeske woorke with a foote of wainscott and the Bellowes lying in the same.

Item. An Instrumente that goethe with a whele without playinge uppon, of woode vernisshed yellowe and painted blewe with vi round plates of siluer pounced with anticke garnisshed with an edge of copper and guilte.

Item. A paire of Claricordes couered with gilte leather.

Item. xix Vialles greate and small with iii cases of woode couered with blacke leather to the same.

Item. One Case furnisshed with xv flutes in it.

Item. vi Recorders of Ivorie in a case of blacke vellat.

Item. One greate base Recorder of woode in a case of woode.

Item. A Baggepipe with pipes of Ivorie, the bagge couered with purple vellat.

Item. Twoo faire paire of newe longe Virginalles made harpe fasshion of Cipres with keies of Ivorie havinge the Kinges armes crowned and supported by his graces beastes within a gartier guilte standinge ouer the saide keies with twoo caeses to them couered with blacke leather the inner partes of the liddes to the saide caeses being of wallnuttre with condrie antickes of white woode wroughte in the same.

AT HAMPTON COURTE

One payre of portatives with the Kynges and Quene Janes Armes.
Seven paires of Virginalles in cases of printed lether.

AT NEWHALL

A paire of faire greate Organes in the Chappell with a curten afore them of lynnen clothe staynd redd and blewe paned.
A paire of Virginalles verye olde and broken.
One olde Lute.

There is something very endearing about the 'olde Lute'. One can see in Henry the ideal that Sir Thomas Elyot recommended in *The Boke Named the Governour*: 'In this commendation of musicke I wold not be thought to allure noble men to have so moche delectation therein, that, in playinge and singynge only, they shulde put their holle studie and felicitie: as dyd the emperour Nero. . . . It suffised a noble man, hauynge therein knowledge either to use it secretely, for the refreshynge of his witte, when he hathe tyme of solace: orels, only hearynge the contention of noble musiciens to give iugement in the excellencie of their counnynges.'

II
BRITANNIA
TRIUMPHANS

Amateur music-making has never been a more requisite social grace than it was in England under the Virgin Queen. With the monarch as model, the power of example was great; with the court as active participants as well as competitive patrons, the political implications of the art were evident; with the rise of that unique spectacle, the court masque, amateur music-making and political propaganda were united as never before or since.

In appreciation of the arts and entertainments, the queen herself set the tone for her courtiers. 'Elizabeth as well as the rest of Henry VIII's children and, indeed, all the princes of Europe of that time had been taught music early in life,' declared Charles Burney from his eighteenth-century viewpoint on English history. More cautiously, he went on: 'there is reason to conclude that she continued to amuse herself with Music many years after she ascended the Throne'. But the evidence of Elizabeth's personal performance proves her to have been a strict adherer to the rules of Elyot, which were the precepts of several writers on courtly characteristics. Music was for private recreation only, and, said Castiglione in *Il Cortegiano*, 'I will have our courtier therefore do this as a matter that is not his profession; and not to seem to seek or look for any praise for it, nor be acknowen that he bestoweth much study or time about it, although he do it excellently well.'

Once the rules of privacy were broken, however, the queen could not conceal her desire to know how her performance compared with that of her royal sister, Mary. When faced with the question of how well the Queen of Scots played on the virginals, Sir James Melville, sent as ambassador from Scotland, replied with commendable presence of mind 'Reasonably — for a Queen'. On his own account, he must have been one of few people in a position to compare the two ladies:

That same day after Dinner my Lord of Hunsdean drew me up to a quiet Gallery, that I might hear some Musick, but he said that he durst now avow it, where I might hear the Queen play upon the Virginals. After I had hearkned awhile, I took by the Tapistry that hung before the door of the Chamber, and seeing her back was toward the door, I entered within the Chamber, and stood a pretty space hearing her play excellently well, but she left off immediately, so soon as she turned her about and saw me. She appeared to be surprized to see me, and came forward, seeming to strike me with her hand, alledging she used not to play before Men, but when she was solitary to shun melancholly. She asked how I came there? I answered, as I was walking with my Lord of Hunsdean, as we past by the Chamber door, I heard such melody as ravished me, whereby I was

20. *Elaborately decorated virginals of Italian construction, traditionally associated with Elizabeth, the Winter Queen of Bohemia. Now in the Victoria and Albert Museum, London.*

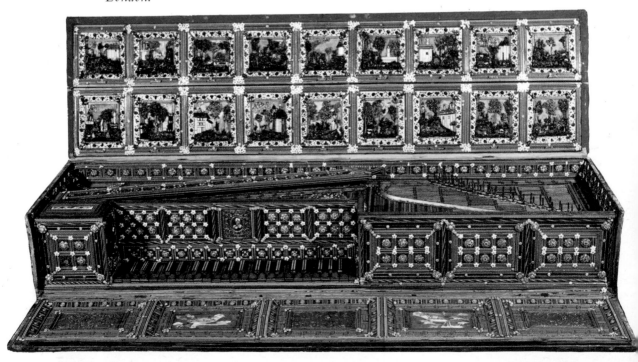

21. *Elizabeth I playing the lute (Nicholas Hilliard)*.

drawn in e're I knew how, excusing my fault of homeliness, as being brought up in the Court of France, where such freedom was allowed; declaring my self willing to endure what kind of punishment her Majesty should be pleased to inflict upon me for so great an offence. Then she sate down low upon a Cushion, and I upon my knees by her, but with her own hand she gave me a Cushion, to lay under my knee, which at first I refused, but she compelled me to take it. She then called for my Lady Strafford out of the next Chamber, for the Queen was alone. She inquired whether my Queen or she played best! In that I found my self obliged to give her the praise.

The queen's vanity was not satisfied even with this compliment; she kept Melville two more days at court purely so that he could see her dance, 'which being over, she inquired of me whether she or my Queen Danced best? I answered, the Queen Danced not so high, and disportedly as she did.'

Dancing was the public court activity *par excellence*, and the queen's enthusiasm for this social and moral form of exercise lasted well into her old age. 'I assure you,' wrote one courtier from the 'warm winter box' of Richmond Palace, 'six or seven gallyards of a mornynge, besydes musycke and syngynge, is her ordinary excercise.' Queens were rivals even in these activities. The famous portrait in Penshurst Place of Elizabeth dancing *La Volta*, supported by Dudley, Earl of Leicester, is in fact an English transposition of an earlier French painting featuring Marguerite de Valois in identical posture. One critic claimed: 'The Voltas which magicians have brought from Italy have this misfortune, that a great many murders and miscarriages result from them.' The energetic leaps involved in this particular dance would have been considered daring for either queen, but Elizabeth was not going to be outdone by any rival, living or dead. Dancing seems to have appealed to her more than the other arts; her support of music, particularly her constant protection of William Byrd despite his recusancy, was commendable and idealistic rather than extravagant.

Her warmest approval was reserved for those displays of loyalty and devotion with which she was entertained on progresses, and in these instances propaganda added to the pleasure of compliment.

22. *William Byrd, from an engraving of* 1719 *by Nicholas Haym.*

It is easy to overlook the fact that almost all examples of the art that we know from this period could more accurately be termed 'London' than 'English' music. Only when the court was on the move would the queen's musicians and the ritual which accompanied them be available to the people outside the capital: hence Elizabeth's calculated enthusiasm for such elaborate revels on tour as the show mounted for her at Elvetham in September 1591. One dance song in particular appealed to her: its music was by Edward Johnson, and its title 'Eliza is the fairest Queen'. 'This spectacle and music so delighted her Majesty that she commanded to hear it sung and to be danced three times over, and called for divers lords and ladies to behold it.' Similarly elaborate displays of religious music were designed to create the most favourable impression on visitors, especially foreigners. Frederick, Duke of Würtemberg, visited Windsor in 1592 and found 'the music, especially the organ, exquisitely played; for at times you could hear the sound of cornets, flutes, then fifes and other instruments; and there was likewise a little boy who sang so sweetly amongst it all, and threw such charm over the music with his little tongue, that it was really wonderful to listen to him.'

Apart from the political expediency attached, Elizabeth was loth to squander money on music, or any other art, merely for entertainment. But the arrival of a suitor justified expenditure: 'The coming of the Duke of *Alenzon* into *England*, opened a way to a more free way of living, and relaxed very much the old severe form of Discipline. The Queen danced often then, and omitted no sort of Recreation. . . . Dances, Masques, and variety of rich Attires, were all taken up, and used, to show him how much he was honoured.' But once he had been sent back to France 'she as heartily endeavoured to reduce her nobility to their old severe way of living'. Her nobility were not so ready to reduce their commitment to the arts; monarchs could create fashion, but their courtiers supplied much of the employment and the continuity that a musician expected.

Although family patronage in Elizabeth's reign was not as widespread as tradition would suggest — Wilbye's life at Hengrave Hall with the Kytson family in Suffolk is the exception rather than the rule — individual commissions and special celebrations were a continual source of employment. Many of the dedications of the greatest collections of Elizabethan music cite the names of most of the country's leading families. Sir William Cecil is complimented by Thomas Robinson in his *New Citharen Lessons* for his grandfather's 'beautifull kindenesse towards my Father . . . and that I alwaies have tasted of the comfortable liberalitie of Your Honours Father' — patronage was a tradition in the Salisbury family. Byrd dedicated a pavan to the memory of Sir William — 'Pavana The Earle of Salisbury' — as did a composer from the new generation, Orlando Gibbons. Household accounts show that few events could pass without the 'musitions' being required. Christmas music, for example, cost the Earl of Rutland £6 13s 4d, although the payments were included in 'wages of servant in the household there as cooks, brewer, baker, catur and such like . . .' Births, weddings, for which 'the violins' were used, and frequent feastings, called for a

23. *'Inigo Jones first brought the theorbo to England c.ann.1605. At Dover it was thought some engine brought from Popish countries to destroy the King, and he had it sent up to Council Table.' The portrait is of Lady Mary Sidney, niece of Sir Philip.*

24. *Marguerite de Valois dancing* La Volta *at the Valois Court.*

25. *Queen Elizabeth and Robert Dudley, Earl of Leicester, in a patently derivative pose (artist unknown).*

small band to be present. Sir William Petre ordered 'a paire of iron brackets to set the double virginals upon the Great Chamber' at Ingatestone where Byrd was a guest for Christmas 1589. The Earl of Essex even took care to have a musician present the night before he died, when 'he willed William Hayes, his musician to play on the virginals, and to sing. "Play" said he, "my song, and I will sing it myself." And so he did most joyfully . . .'

In the elaborate mural recording the wedding feast of Sir Henry Unton, the queen's ambassador in France, an ensemble of musicians accompanies the wedding masque and matches in every detail the innovatory prescription of Thomas Morley's *Consort Lessons* of 1599 for 'sixe Instruments to play together: viz. the treble lute, the Pandora, the Citterne, the base-viol, the flute and the treble-viol'. These arrangements of works by 'divers exquisite Authors' were the first attempts to provide a repertoire in print for instruments other than the lute and the keyboard. As the possibilities of publishing music improved, so did the composer's interest in tempting the aristocratic market. Title pages described

26. *Detail from a mural painted c.1596, showing the wedding feast of Sir Henry Unton, with the masquers making an entry up the stairs.*

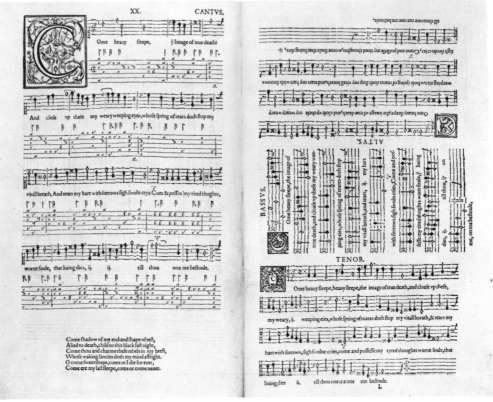

27. *'Come heavy sleepe' from John Dowland's* First Booke of Songes, *published in* 1597 *with a dedication to Lord Hunsdon. The left-hand page contains the soprano line and lute part in tablature; the remaining vocal parts are printed on the right-hand page so that a single book can be read by four performers seated round a table.*

music as suitable for any occasion, 'apt for viols, violins or other musical wind instruments' or simply 'very easie to be performed'. No doubt Michael East, albeit unwittingly, expressed the true state of aristocratic competence when in the dedication of his *Second Set of Madrigals* he commended Sir Thomas Gerard's 'perfection in music . . . rare in a gentleman of your rank'.

The fickle nature of English patronage explains the sporadic development of many musical styles during the late sixteenth century in England. The madrigal, for example, imported as a new fashion from Italy along with *Musica Transalpina*, flowered and died as quickly as Shakespeare's theatre. English keyboard music, brought to perfection in the works of Byrd and his fellow-virginalists, decayed and left only lightweight successors. The English consort style succumbed to the vogue for exotica, a victim of what Morley called 'the new-fangled opinions of our countrymen who will highly esteem whatsoever cometh from beyond the seas (and specially from Italy) be it never so simple, condemning that which is done at home though it be never so excellent'.

'Long live fair Oriana' was the hopeful refrain of the collection of madrigals designed for the queen under the editorship of Morley; when *The Triumphes of*

Oriana was published in 1603, the contributors had to adapt their final line to read 'In heaven now lives fair Oriana'. The queen, who had reduced the size and expenditure of her household music well below that of her father, who had refused employment to John Dowland, the most acclaimed instrumentalist of his day, who had employed four foreigners for every Englishman in her *Musicke,*★ and who initiated laws to include minstrels in the penalties devised for vagabonds (branding on first conviction and death on the third) — this queen was dead. Her reputation now passed into the hands of the eulogists; the fiction of Spenser's *The Faerie Queene* was built to last.

James I was not so fortunate. Our impressions of his character come from hostile contemporaries, would-be courtiers disappointed of office, or rejected suitors. No English monarch has ever had more need of a public relations office. But despite our inclinations to back-date the Golden Age, it was with Stuart money and under Stuart patronage that the finest English arts flourished at court. James was not the most musical of monarchs, but he understood the political power of spectacle, and was convinced that as God's representative on earth, he should encourage the arts to broadcast this image. For a king it was more important that his patronage should be visible, rather than that he should be able to indulge his own tastes in private. Employing the individuality of skills surrounding the court, James and his foreign wife put their greatest support behind the court masque — the first fully political realization in England of the power of the arts.

The Tudor court had established a tradition of mumming and masquerades, entertainments with slight symbolic purposes, which were the main ingredient of the Revels at Shrovetide and Christmas. Civic pageantry and the ritual of the tournaments were more politically significant, establishing the important fact that the participants were the courtiers themselves, disguised as heroes of antiquity, but playing no deeper part. Under the aspect of nymphs, shepherds and assorted deities, they played out their real obligations to the monarch: in the guise of Oberon, Prince of Faery, or Pan, the universal god, princes could embody in action the theories of kingship in which they believed.

Such was the theory. In practice, however, things were not always so apparent. The masque itself was essentially a form of amateur theatricals, much glamorized and held together by professional organization. Sir John Harington, a godson of Elizabeth I and one of James's rejected suitors, gave a jaundiced account of the entertainment offered by James to his brother-in-law, the alcoholic Christian IV, and his Danish retinue on a visit to England in 1606. One day a great feast was held, and after dinner the representation of Solomon his Temple and the coming of the Queen of Sheba was made, or, as I may better

★ The families of Bassano, Lupo, Lanier and Ferrabosco dominated the next fifty years of English music.

say, was meant to have been made, before their Majesties, by device of the Earl of Salisbury and others. But alas! as all earthly things do fail to poor mortals in enjoyment, so did prove our presentment hereof. The Lady who did play the Queen's part did carry most precious gifts to both their Majesties; but forgetting the steppes arising to the canopy, overset her caskets into his Danish Majesties lap, and fell at his feet, tho I rather think it was in his face. Much was the hurry and confusion; cloths and napkins were at hand to make all clean. His Majesty then got up and would dance with the Queen of Sheba; but he fell down and humbled himself before her, and was carried to an inner chamber and laid on a bed of state; which was not a little defiled with the presents of the Queen which had been bestowed on his garments; such as wine, cream, jelly, beverage, cakes, spices and other good matters. The entertainment and shew went forward and most of the presenters went backward, or fell down, wine did so occupy their upper chambers. Now did appear in rich dress, Hope, Faith and Charity: Hope did assay to speak, but wine rendered her endeavours so feeble that she

28. *Lucy Russell (née Harington), Countess of Bedford, a close friend of Elizabeth of Bohemia and Anne of Denmark, in costume for Ben Jonson's masque* Hymenaei, 1606.

withdrew, and hoped the King would excuse her brevity. Faith was then all alone, for I am certain she was not joyned with good works; and left the Court in a staggering condition. Charity came to the Kings feet, and seemed to cover the multitude of sins her sisters had committed: In some sorte she made obeysance and brought giftes, but said she would return home again, as there was no gift which Heaven had not already given his Majesty; she then returned to Hope and Faith, who were both sick and spewing in the lower hall. Next came *Victory*, in bright armour, and presented a rich sword to the King, who did not accept it, but put it by with his hand; and by a strange medley of versification, did endeavour to make suit to the King; but Victory did not tryumph for long, for, after much lamentable utterance, she was led away like a silly captive, and laid to sleep in the outer steps of the anti-chamber. Now did Peace make entry, and strive to get foremoste to the King; but I grieve to tell how great wrath she did discover unto those of her attendants, and, much contrary to her own semblance, most rudely made war with her olive branch, and laid on the pates of those who did oppose her coming. I have much marvelled at these strange pageantries, and they do bring to my remembrance what passed of this sort in our Queens days: of which I was sometime an humble presenter and assistant; but I neer did see such lack of good order, discretion and sobreity, as I have now done. . . .

Remembering Hamlet's comments on the drunkenness of the Danish court, it may be that James's visitors were familiar with such disasters. Despite set-backs James made good use of the power of the masque on occasions of political importance, gathering together a team of artists, designers, poets, musicians and dancers who worked in uneasy harmony to reconcile the disparate elements of the form.

> Oh Showes! Showes! Mighty Showes!
> The Eloquence of Masques! What need of prose
> Or Verse, or Sense t'Express Immortall you?
> You are the Spectacles of State!

Ben Jonson, the creator of so many masque texts, insisted on the power of the 'remov'd mysteries', the 'mirror of man's life', which were, for him, at the heart of masque. For Inigo Jones, the designer of the costumes, sets and machines, Jonson's close collaborator on many masques, and eventually his bitterest enemy, these shows were 'nothing else but Pictures and Light and Motion'. Music was rarely mentioned, and a feature of this overwhelming form is that the masque never came to terms with the world of Italian opera; music was one component of an entertainment that attempted to synthesize spectacle, words and dance.

The shows were presented by the court for the court, in the Banqueting Hall (or, while that was being rebuilt, in the Great Hall of Whitehall) usually at Twelfth Night, or in celebration of a noble marriage. The king, seated on a raised platform at the centre of the tiers of spectators, held the only ideal position from which to view the perspective lines of the sets. Around him sat the court, separated from the masquers' world of Inigo Jones's baroque devices. As the masque proceeded, further depths to the set were revealed in still grander transformations, until at the end, the process was reversed and the masquers came forward from the stage onto the hall floor, to draw the court into the ultimate dance.

For many spectators the visual aspect was most exciting. Some fortunate guests were invited to see the sets prior to the performance, when the various machines would be demonstrated to them. Campion's *Lord Haye's Masque* required the transformation of the Knights of Apollo into 'goulden trees set in a double vale, so artifically painted, that it seemed as if darke cloudes had hung before it'. When sylvan music sounded, these trees were found to be dancing together. 'Presently the Silvans with their foure instruments and five voices began to play and sing together, at the beginning whereof that part of the stage whereon the first trees stoode began to yeeld, and the three foremost trees gently to sincke, and this was effected by an Ingin plac't under the stage. When the trees had sunke a yarde they cleft in three parts, and the Maskers appeared out of the tops of them.' All this was to have taken place to the accompaniment of a 'Songe

29. *One of the triumphal arches erected to welcome the* Winter King and Queen *to* Oppenheim. *It is possible that Inigo Jones accompanied this progress in the train of the Earl of Arundel.*

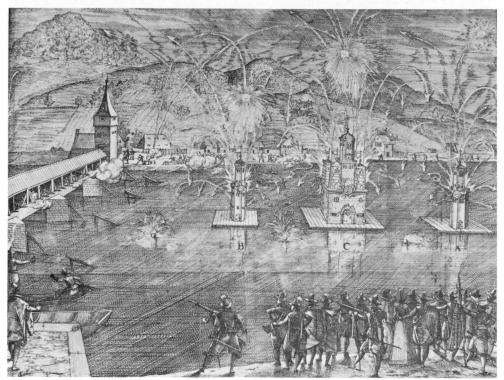

30. *The firework display that greeted the Winter King and Queen on their arrival at Heidleberg, in June* 1613.

of Transformation', but, wrote Campion accusingly, 'either by the simplicity, negligence, or conspiracy of the painter, the passing away of the trees was somewhat hazarded; the patterne of them the same day having bene showne with much admiration, and the 9 trees beeing left unsett together even to the same night'. Presumably some stage-hand forgot to reconnect them to the 'Ingin'.

Occasionally the masque texts described the consorts of music required: 'This Chorus was in the manner of an Eccho seconded by the Cornets, then by the consort of ten, then by the consorte of twelve . . . On the right hand, ten Musitions, with Basse and Meane lutes, a Bandora, double Sackbott, and an Harpsicord, with two treble Violins; on the other side . . . 9 Violins and three Lutes; and to answere both the Consorts (as it were in a triangle) six Cornets, and six Chappel voyces, in a place raised higher in respect of the pearcing sound of those Instruments.' (*Lord Haye's Masque.*) Francis Bacon, who was responsible for mounting and financing several diplomatic masques would have approved the 'pearcing sounds': masques and triumphs are, he said, 'but Toyes . . . yet, since Princes will have such Things, it is better, they should be Graced with Elegancy, than Daubed with Cost. . . . The *Voices* of the *Dialogue*, would be Strong and Manly, (A Base, and a Tenour; No Treble) And the Ditty High and Tragicall; Not nice or Dainty. Let the *Songs* be *Loud*, and *Cheerefull*, and not

Chirpings or *Pulings.* Let the *Musicke* likewise, be *Sharpe*, and *Loud*, and *Well Placed.* But enoughe of these Toyes.'

Bacon's curt dismissal may very well have been occasioned by a disaster that befell one of his own productions at the important celebrations marking the marriage of James's daughter Elizabeth to Frederick, Elector Palatine. This teenage match of Winter King and Winter Queen on St Valentine's Day 1612 was accompanied by every form of spectacle the king could devise. Shakespeare as leading writer for the King's Men came forward with *The Tempest* — possibly the nuptial masque was specially designed for this performance. The Elector was invested with the Order of the Garter, and entertained with an elaborate firework display depicting St George attacking the Dragon 'with reports thwacking and lights burning' — the explosions unfortunately injuring several of the spectators. The wedding ceremony itself, with elaborate anthems, including one by the princess's music teacher John Bull, took place in the Chapel Royal at Whitehall; six German trumpeters preceded Frederick, their fanfares exciting the crowds to shouts of 'God give them joy'.

On the wedding evening the first of three masques was given: *The Lords' Masque,* with words by Campion, for which he was paid £66 13s 4d, and designs by Inigo Jones, at a cost of £50. The main dancers received either £30 or £40, while the musicians Giovanni Coprario★, Robert Johnson and Thomas Lupo got £10 or £20. The remainder of the players, some forty-two, plus ten members of the king's violins, each got £1. As with so much of the music from these ephemeral entertainments, very little has survived to give us much idea of the magnificence of the instrumentation, although the theme of the first scenes, the power of Orpheus' music to charm madness, clearly depended on musical effects:

At the sound of a strange musicke twelve Franticks enter, six men and six women, all presented in sundry habits and humours: in middest of whom Entheus (or Poeticke furie) was hurried forth, and tost up and downe, till by vertue of a new change in the musicke, the Lunatickes fell into a madde measure, fitted to a loud phantasticke tune; but in the end thereof the musicke changed into a very solemne ayre, which they softly played, while Orpheus spake.

The eventual harmony of the spheres at the end, and the symbolic unification of the Rhine and the Thames, called forth Inigo Jones's most elaborate machinery to date. To the accompaniment of a song, 'Advance your Chorall motions now, You musick-loving lights', 'the Starres mooved in an exceeding strange and delightfull maner; and I suppose fewe have ever seen more neate artifice then Master Innigoe Jones shewed in contriving their Motion, who in all the rest of the workmanship which belong'd to the whole invention shewed

★ He had been born plain John Cooper, in Greenwich.

31. *Copy of a miniature of Elizabeth and Frederick of Bohemia, and their son.*

extraordinarie industrie and skill; about the end of this Song, the Starres suddaincly vanished, as if they had beene drowned amongst the Cloudes, and the eight Maskers appeared in their habits, which were infinitly rich, befitting States (such as indeede they all werc), as also a time so farre heightned the day before with all the richest shew of solemnitie that could be invented.'

Some of the audience were bored by the length of this production John Chamberlain complained to Sir Dudley Carleton: 'that night was the lord's mask, whereof I hear no great commendation, save only for riches, their devices being long and tedious, and more like a play than a mask.'

But this was nothing to the sad events that befell the masque presented by the Inner Temple and Gray's Inn on the following night, the production for which Sir Francis had spared 'no time nor travail in the setting forth, ordering and furnishing'. His scheme of arrival was contrived to continue the metaphor of the unification of the Thames and the Rhine, the masquers making their way to the Temple Star by water, starting from Southwark. But, as Sir John Chamberlain recorded, the cleverest plans go awry.

Their shew by water was very gallant by reason of infinite store of lights very curiously set and placed; and many boats and barges with devices of light of lamps with three peals of ordnance, one at their taking water, another in the Temple-garden, and the last at their landing; which passage by water cost them better than £300. They were received at the Privy Stairs; a great expectation there was that they should every way excel their competitors that went before them, both in devise, daintiness of apparel, and, above all, in dancing, wherein they are held excellent, and esteemed the properer men. But by what ill planet it fell out, I know not; they came home as they went without doing anything; the reason whereof I cannot yet learn thoroughly, but only that the Hall was so full that it was not possible to avoid it, or make room for them; besides that most of the Ladies were in the Galleries to see them land, and could not get in. But the worst of all was, that the King was so wearied and sleepy with setting up almost two whole nights before, that he had no edge to it. Whereupon, Sir Francis Bacon ventured to entreat his Majesty, that by this disgrace he would not as it were bury them quick; and I hear the King should answer, that then they must bury him quick, for he could last no longer; but withall gave them very good words, and appointed them to come again on Saturday. But the grace of the Mask is quite gone, when their apparel hath been already showed, and their devices vented, so that how it will fall out God knows; for they are much discouraged and out of countenance, and the world says it comes to pass after the old proverb, 'the properer men the worse luck'.

The king made good his bad manners, however, by commending the performance when it eventually took place, and the music was judged very effective: 'The Statues enter, and at their coming, the musick changed from

32. *Title-page of* Parthenia. *The engraving, however, is an adaptation of an earlier Dutch print showing St Caecelia playing the organ.*

violins to hautboys, cornets, &c. and the air of the musick was utterly turned into a soft time, with drawing notes, excellently expressing their natures. The musick was extremely well-fitted, having such a spirit of country jollity as can hardly be imagined; but the perpetual laughter and applause was above the musick.' James so enjoyed the statue scene that at the end of the performance he called for it again; 'but one of the Statues by that time was undressed'.

When the young couple finally made their departure from Gravesend the musical offering that they took with them was, however, associated with none of the masque performances. A collection of keyboard music by the three most distinguished living composers, William Byrd, John Bull and Orlando Gibbons had been specially printed under the punning title of *Parthenia, or The Maydenhead of the first musicke that ever was printed for the Virginalls*, containing twenty-one of the best examples of English writing from three generations — Byrd was 68, Bull nearly 50, while Gibbons ('the best Finger of that age') was still in his twenties. It was the first music to have been printed from engraved copper plates *in England* (Italy and Germany had anticipated this development) and there could have been no better summary of the age to offer the married couple: from Byrd's memories of his friend Sir William Petre, and his pavan for the Earl of Salisbury, through the virtuosity of John Bull's dances to the sombre melodiousness of Gibbons' 'Fantazia' and the out-going compliment of his bravura variations aptly entitled 'The Queen's Command'.

George Chapman wrote the commendatory poem for the collection:

> In worthy love of this new worck
> and the most Autenticall Aucthors.

> By theis choice lessons of theise Musique Mast^{rs}:
>   Ancient, and heightn'd wth ye Arts full Bowles,
> Let all ou^r moderne, mere Phantastique Tasters,
>   (Whose Art but forreigne Noveltie extolls)
> Rule and confine theyr fancies; and prefer
>   The constant right & depthe Art should pduce
> To all lite flashes, by whose light they err;
>   This wittie Age, hath wisedome least in use;
> The world, ould growing, Ould, wth it, grow Men,
>   Theyr skylls decaying, like theyr bodies streng^{the};
> Young Men, to oulde are now but Childeren:
>   First Rules of Art, encrease still wththeyr leng^{the}.
> Which see in this new worck, yet never seene:
>   Art y^e more oulde, growes ev^r y^e more greene.

III
LE ROI SOLEIL

As the final scene of *La Ballet de la Nuit* drew to a close on 23 February 1653 the audience in the Petit Bourbon were treated to a last transformation devised by Torelli, the 'Great Wizard' of stage scene design in seventeenth century France.

Dawn pulls a superb chariot bringing the most beautiful Sun that one had ever seen, which at first dissipated the clouds and then promised the most beautiful and the greatest Day of the World; the Spirits came to render him homage, and that formed the *grand Ballet*. The *sujet* is vast and in all of its Extensiveness completely worthy to exercise the steps of our Young Monarch, without detracting from the scheme. . . .

For the audience that night, many of whom had queued for five or six hours to see the performance, it was the first time that their king, the young Louis XIV, had appeared before them as the 'rising sun'. The symbolism was not missed, and, reluctantly as Louis took to it, it was to be a motif that heralded him throughout his life, and a nickname that has dogged him ever since.

For another performer that evening was equally significant. Although he had taken charge of one of the *entrées* himself, revising the music, instructing the players and even advising the king on the most suitable steps and coaching him in his part, Giovanni-Battista Lully, only twenty years old, was far from being a French nobleman. Born in Florence (some said the son of a miller), he made his way to France with a reputation as a dancer, and gained a nominal position in the household of Mlle de Montpensier, the king's cousin, as *valet de chambre* and teacher of Italian. *La Grande Mademoiselle* made very slow progress in Italian, and when she was confined to the Tuileries in 1652, she recalled releasing Lully 'because he was a great dancer'. Curiously enough she did not mention his violin playing, although there seems to be some truth in the tale that he was overheard entertaining the servants in the kitchen with a brisk *branle* on the violin, and reported back to mademoiselle as 'the best violinist in Paris'.

Lully was also a wit, a born entertainer, a mimic, an excellent dancer, a pederast and a *libertin*: he became the most powerful musician and impressario in France, one of the closest friends of Europe's greatest monarch, a successful property developer and a notoriously loose-living member of a society already dissipated and scandalously unorthodox. This '*plus grande Journée du Monde*', as he himself described it, took place almost entirely within the confines of the royal theatre and its world of '*spectacles et magnifices*'; it was a career undertaken at hazard, risking the loss of royal patronage or an alteration in '*le grand goût*' of the king. Yet even when others were out of favour and when serious opera was sneered at, Lully survived with approval. Madame de Sévigné was so affected by *Alceste* ('*un prodigue de beauté*') that she could not restrain her tears; but, she was quick to add, she was not alone in this: '*L'âme de Mme de la Fayette en est alarmée*'. Even the jaundiced St Evremond, satiated by a superfluity of spectacle during his days in England, had to except Lully from his general denigration of opera.

Would you know what an opera is? I'll tell you, it is an odd medley of Poetry and Musick, wherein the Poet and Musician, equally confined one by the other, take a World of Pains to compose a wretched Performance. . . . It remains that I give my advice in general for all Comedies where any singing is used; and that is to

33. *Jean-Baptiste Lully.*

leave to the Poet's discretion the management of the Piece. The Musician is to follow the Poet's direction, only in my opinion, Lully is to be exempted, who knows the passions and enters further into the Heart of the man than the Authors themselves.

Spectacle was still the main component of courtly art when Lully arrived in Paris. In a tradition of '*magnifices*' that stretched back to the time of Catherine de' Medici and the Valois court, political *fêtes* had maintained extravagant links between classical themes and contemporary politics. The Valois tapestries preserve in detail the colourfulness of these occasions, the Queen Mother looking on in her widow's weeds. She was proud of the skill with which she arranged the political as well as the spectacular aspects of these fêtes, and several of the themes of which she was most fond recur in later French art. In addition to the expected exotica (an elephant scene, for instance, or the arrival of a whale in the festival at Bayonne) peasant dances were used to represent the restoration of peace, anticipating many of the pastoral devices that were such a feature of the Versailles ballets. Catherine's daughter, Marguerite de Valois, commented on such a pastoral episode in the water fête of Bayonne:

These shepherdesses, during the passage of the superb boats from Bayonne to the island, were placed in separate bands, in a meadow on each side of the causeway, raised with turf. . . . After landing, the shepherdesses I have mentioned before received the company in separate troops, with sinop and dances, after the fashion and accompanied by the music of the provinces they represented — the Poiterins playing on bagpipes; the Provençales on the viol and cymbal; the Burgundians and Champagners on the hautboy, bass viol, and tambourine; in like manner the Bretons and other provincialists. After the collation was served and the feast at an end, a large troop of musicians, habited like satyrs, were seen to come out of the opening of a rock, well lighted up, whilst nymphs were descending from the top in rich habits, who, as they came down, formed into a grand dance . . .

In all these '*spectacles*' and '*magnificences*', dancing was the most important courtly element in which the political protagonists were expected to take part — as was also the case with the more restrained English masques of the seventeenth century. It is reported that Marguerite herself was so notable an exponent of the *volta* that on hearing a description of her performance, the Governor of the Netherlands rode post haste to Paris to see it with his own eyes.

　　The harmony expressed in organized movement and sound in these *spectacles* symbolized political euphony, and by the following century the dance was the most perfect vehicle for representing the absolutism of *le grand monarque*. Catherine de' Medici created the *ballet de cour*, the most expensive involvement

34. *Louis XIV as 'Le Roi Soleil' in* La Ballet de la Nuit, 1653.

35. *Catherine de' Medici (in black) looking on at the court ball following the* Ballet of the Provinces of France, 1573. *(The Valois Tapestries).*

of the court and the arts of the following century, with such fêtes as *Le Paradis d'Amour.* In the *Ballet of the Provinces of France* the Queen Mother and sixteen other ladies danced for an hour in a hall blazing with flambeaux, the grandeur of which sight 'could not possibly be imitated by any king on earth'. When setting up the first of his Royal Academies, the *Academie de Danse*, Louis XIV declared that 'the art of dance has always been recognized as one of the most respectable and necessary to train the body and to give it the first and most natural dispositions to every kind of exercise, to that of the arms among others. Consequently, it is one of the most advantageous and useful to our nobility, and to others who have the honour of approaching us, not just in wartime in our armies, but even in times of peace in the *divertissement* of our ballets.' Louis was merely restating what had been commonly accepted during the earlier part of the century — that the three skills of a nobleman should be riding, dancing and fencing. To them, if not to us, all three implied military utility as well as grace and display.

In the *ballets de cour* it was necessary for the nobility to show as much aptitude as they had done in the obligatory 'tourneys' and jousts of the Valois court. Saint-Hubert, who gave practical instructions on *La manière de composer et faire réussir les ballets* emphasized that 'it is very necessary to take time to study the steps and *entrées*'. He added, presumably for those of the nobility too arrogant or lazy to take the necessary exercise: 'That which is improvised never succeeds well; fifteen days for a *grand ballet* and eight days for a *petit ballet* would not be too much time to spend in preparation.' In just such a *spectacle* Lully found himself dancing next to *Le Roi Soleil*, and from that encounter he proceeded to apply for the post of *Compositeur de la Musique Instrumentale* when the elderly Lazarin died: naturally he was successful.

His control now extended over the famous band of strings that had been set up by Louis' father to provide music at court, the *Vingt-quatre Violons du Roi*, which served as a training ground for the most brilliant players in France, and established a stylized method of playing dance music. Lully did not think much of this ensemble. He disliked their exclusiveness, and criticized their manner of decorating and embellishing everything they played. Since they performed from memory the results were often disastrous. In retaliation, he set up the *Petits Violons*, a smaller group of his own choosing, which was to spread his fame as an orchestral trainer. They were required to play for the king at dinner and as he went to bed. That they pleased him is evident since he paid for them from a separate fund usually reserved for the ceremonial trumpeters. In this band there was '*point de broderie*', the style, with its rapid *tirades* and aggressive dotted rhythms was simple, but dramatic and affecting. The type of overture that Lully evolved with these playing techniques in mind provided a model for the remainder of the baroque age. In England Roger North reported that 'all the compositions of the town were strained to imitate Baptist's vein', and Pelham Humfrey, sent over to France by Charles II to absorb the new idiom, returned full of Lully's style, and (said Pepys) 'an absolute Monsieur'. Manners as well as music were showing signs of change, and it was not only the composers who needed to turn to the French to acquire something of 'Gayety and Fashion', as Purcell put it.

The institutions of France — the reforms of Colbert, the buildings of Versailles, the formal gardens, even the language of the *précieuses* (described by Wilfred Mellers as 'the ultimate inability to call a spade a spade') — were seized upon as evidence that, in their values and standards, the French had achieved a unity of sensibility and civilisation which had escaped the rest of Europe. With the Sun King as his focal point, every citizen could find some parable or analogy

36. 'Country musicians' from the ballet Les Feés des forêtsSaint Germain, 1625. All lutes, with the exception of one viol, held in a somewhat unusual position.

around him to confirm the absolutism of the monarchy, be it the geometrical layout of the parks and gardens of Versailles, arranged so that the main axis of the design should pass through the king's bedchamber, the poise and serenity of Poussin's paintings, the elegant wit of Molière's theatre, or the sumptuous display of Lully's ballets. Every citizen was admitted to this greatest of all palaces, and allowed to wander at will through the marble halls, hung with mirrors, the sole stipulation being that, to prove he was a gentleman, he should wear a sword. With typical practicality swords could be hired at the door by any visitor in need.

Patronage had to be sophisticated in so rarified a setting if it were to reflect well on the patron. 'His Majesty, loving the fine arts as much as he does, will cultivate them with even greater care that they may serve to immortalize his great and glorious actions' summarized Colbert and promptly set about organizing the component parts of the king's artistic empire into *Académies*. Painting, sculpture, dance, literature, science, music and architecture were systematized, in that order, reflecting the importance he thought they could play in increasing '*la gloire*'. The king himself was hardly a performing musician; the full extent of his practical talents was that he accompanied Louise de la Vallière on the guitar while she sang to him. In selecting his musicians, however, he showed great acuteness.

He himself chose musical tutors for the royal family; he suggested themes for operas to Lully and Quinault; he presented Clérambault with texts for cantatas; and he ran competitions to choose *sous-maîtres* for his chapel who could 'acquit themselves of their duties perfectly'.

The *Musiciens du Roi* were organized with the same precision. Lully had control of the *Musique de Chambre*, a group which ostensibly included both the *Vingt-quatre Violons* and the *Petite Bande*, although these ensembles were virtually autonomous. The division of labour between the two groups is hard to define, although the *Etat de France* of 1686 declared:

The *Grande Bande* of the *Vingt-quatre Violons*, always so labelled although they are at present twenty-five . . . plays for the dinner of the King, for Ballets and for Comedies. The *Petits Violons* which number twenty-four . . . follow the King on his journeys to the country, usually play for his supper, for Balls and the Recreation of His Majesty. They also play for Ballets. . . .

The *Musique de la Chapelle Royale*, where Delalande was resident composer, supplied the *grands motets* that Louis considered the most impressive accompani-

37. *Design by Torelli ('The Great Wizard') for the ballet* Thetis, *showing a typical use of exaggerated perspective.*

ment for his religious services. Marc-Antione Charpentier, as *Maitre de Musique des Enfants* at Sainte-Chapelle, controlled the choir. The third division of Louis' musicians, *La Musique de la Grande Ecurie*, 'music of the great stable', was an impressive band of wind and brass players, whose duties had extended from the original idea of supplying musical accompaniments for outdoor pageantry to serving as the basis of the wind section of the opera orchestra when required. Trumpeters and oboists were basic to ceremonial music, and these players can be seen in the engravings of Louis' coronation procession.

But these traditional engagements did not stifle inventiveness within the ranks of the *12 Grands Hautbois*, actually a select group of ten oboes and two bassoons. Jean Hotteterre and Michael Philidor were woodwind players and makers with an inventive turn of mind, and under the unwitting patronage of Louis, they were experimenting with improvements to the shawm, recorder and flute. Michael de la Barre, one of the players later to achieve fame as a flautist in the king's *Musique de Chambre*, wrote that Lully's elevation had meant the downfall

38. *The symmetry of Versailles in a painting by Pierre-Denis Martin of* 1722.

39. *Jean Berain's design for the enchanted palace in the last act of Lully's* Armide *in 1686; the engines were put in motion, and the palace was destroyed by a conflagration (setting a trend for many other opera finales of this period).*

of all the old instruments except the oboe, 'thanks to Philidor and Hotteterre, who spoiled great quantities of wood and played great quantities of music until they finally succeeded in making the instrument fit for concert use'.

Their concert use is best demonstrated by the elaborate wind parts that Lully included in all his later operas (he had extracted an opera monopoly from the king in 1672), and the extent to which the symbolic use of oboes and flutes influenced baroque music in general testifies to the importance of the Hotteterre and Philidor families. Without their improved instruments we would also be without the pastoral flute solos in Handel, and the characterization of bucolic and rustic texts in Bach with the sound of the oboe. We no longer have the ability to react to many of these symbolic associations in the same way as the seventeenth and eighteenth century listener. Unlike Lully's audience we cannot transfer the notion of earthly kingship to that of theatrical regality via the sound of the royal trumpets. They were much helped by the fact that the trumpeters who played during the opera were the same performers who had supplied the ceremonial fanfares for the entrance of Le Roi Soleil. The sound of the rustic bagpipe or the shepherd flute was not yet so far removed from the more sophisticated professional instrument that the implications of an oboe or flute solo would go unappreciated. Such symbolism was part of the natural language of Bach and Handel, and has only been lost in recent years, obliterated by the anonymity that the modern orchestra requires of its component parts.

40. *A tableau of acrobatic savages by Henry Gissey, designer of the King's ballets from* 1660 *to* 1673.

To Lully and his contemporaries such associations were free from the taint of preciosity that they have acquired in our eyes; affectation had not yet ousted association. When we consider the plots that Lully was offered for the creation of his operas, sycophancy would seem to be their overriding quality, although there is no doubt that a courtier would have accepted the fulsomeness of the flattery more willingly. Courtiers were given three bits of advice: 'Speak well of everyone, ask for everything that's going, and sit down when you get the chance.'

Louis was presented in the guise of Bellérophon, Amadis or Phaeton, as the victorious warrior, the gallant lover — with guarded references to the displacement of Mme de Maintenon — and the benevolent peacemaker. When Lully was offered the subject of Persée by the king himself, the effusiveness of his compliments seems appalling to us: 'You yourself, Sire, have even condescended to make the choice, and as soon as I cast my eyes on it, I discovered the Image of Your Majesty. I understand that in describing the favourable Gifts which Persée has received from the Gods and the astonishing enterprises which he has achieved so gloriously, I am tracing a Portrait of the heroic qualities and wonderful deeds of Your Majesty.' In Lully's defence, the majority of prefaces directed at the king were equally obsequious, and the language if anything more extravagant. On being complimented for his own part in one performance, the composer stated his intentions a little more honestly: 'But Sire, I would aim to be the secretary of the King!'

Lully led a charmed life; despite court intrigues, widespread lampoons and the revelation of an affair with his page, Brunet, his effrontery was successful. On 29 December 1681, for a payment of 60,000 livres (an indication of the wealth he had already accumulated), he was made counsellor-secretary and celebrated his advancement to the nobility with a banquet. 'This evening,' Le Cerf reported, 'there were twenty-five or thirty who, by right, had the best seats: in order that the chancellors could be seen in a body, two or three lines of solemn citizens, wearing evening dress and great beaver hats, were seated in the first rows of the amphitheatre and listened with an admirable seriousness to the minuets and the gavottes of their colleague, the musician.'

While many of the nobility took offence at the arrival of an ex-scullion in their ranks, Le Cerf, Lord of Freneuse, was emphatic in his praise. In his *Comparison of Italian and French Music* of 1705, he took Lully's side against the advocates of Italian bravura; curiously, no-one seems to have pointed out that Lully himself was from Italy. In the conversation between a certain Mademoiselle M—— and Le Chevalier, he was quick to defend the validity of the king's taste in music and Lully's contribution to it.

In the matter of taste, mademoiselle, great nobles are only men like ourselves, whose name proves little. Each has his voice and the voices are equal, or at least it is not their quality which will determine their weight. But in case you put your trust in authorities, we have one on our side to whom you can defer. The King is on our side. But I am no courtier. I do not wish to stress that name, however great it may be, or to maintain that it decides. Let us put aside from the person of the King all the splendour which his rank and his reign bestow upon it, and let us regard him only as a private person in his kingdom. It is only rendering him the justice which one would not refuse to a minister out of favour to say that of all the men of Europe he is one of those born with the greatest sense and most direct and just intelligence. He loves music and is a competent judge of it. The great number of ballets in which he has danced and of operas composed expressly for him or of his choice, the honour he has done to Lully and to so many other musicians in permitting them to approach him, attest that he loves music. That he is a good judge of it, this same love of the art, his familiarity with it, and the personal qualities that no one could refuse to concede that he possesses, are the proof. It is certain that the fashion of hailing with rapture the beauty of the operatic pieces now brought to us from Italy in bales has not yet reached him. Even in Lully's lifetime the King enjoyed a beautiful Italian piece when one was presented to him. He had a motet of Lorenzani sung before him five times. He had, as he still has, among his singers some castrati, in order to have them sing airs from time to time, a thing in which I agree that they are excellent. But for all that he was attached to the opera of Lully, to the music and musicians of France, and since the death of Lully he has not changed his taste; he has stoutly adhered to it, though there have been attempts to make him change it.

If the recent story which a thousand persons have been telling is true, it is specific and shows very well that the magnificence and the lively pace of the Italian symphonies have failed to please him. Don't you know the story, ladies? A courtier of some importance who had extolled these symphonies to the King, brought him a little Batiste, a French violinist of surprising natural aptitude who had studied for three or four years under Corelli. He played rapid passages which would have made Mademoiselle faint with delight or terror before Madame gave the word. The King listened with all the attention that Italy could desire, and when Italy waited to be admired, said, 'Send for one of my violinists!' One came; his name is not given; apparently it was one of mediocre merit, who happened to be at hand.

'An air from *Cadmus*,' said the King.

The violinist played the first one that occurred to him, a simple, unified air;

41. *Court musicians in* 1688, *painted by Pierre Puget. The baroque lute contrasts with the guitar on the table, and the fretted neck of the viol (extreme left) with the unfretted string bass on the right.*

42. *Classical affectation; Louis XIV and his family portrayed in the Roman manner by Jean Nocret.*

and *Cadmus* is not, of all our operas, that from which one would have chosen to select an air if the incident had been premeditated.

'I can only say to you, sir,' said the King to the courtier, 'that is my taste; that is my taste.'

Other commentators of the time were not so ready to award the palm to Lully: 'The Italians are more bold and hardy in their airs than the French,' declared Raguenet, 'they carry their point farther, both in their tender songs and in those that are more sprightly as well as in their other compositions; nay, they often unite styles, which the French think incompatible. It is not to be wondered that the Italians think our music dull and stupefying, that according to their taste it appears flat and insipid, if we consider the nature of the French airs compared to those of the Italian. The French, in their airs, aim at the soft, the easy, the flowing and coherent. But the Italians venture the boldest cadences and the most irregular dissonance; and their airs are so out of the way that they resemble the compositions of no other nation in the world. The French would think themselves undone if they offended in the least against the rules; they flatter, tickle, and court the ear and are still doubtful of success, though everything be done with an exact regularity. The Italians venture at everything that is harsh and out of the way, but then they do it like people that have a right to venture and are sure of success.'

Lully did not survive to see the end of these hostilities; while conducting a Te Deum to celebrate the king's recovery from sickness, he injured his foot with the long staff used as a baton, and died of gangrene poisoning. His epitaph (which can still be seen in Notre-Dame des Victoires in Paris) described him as 'famous for the high degree of perfection he has shown in his beautiful songs and symphonies, who has won the good will of Louis le Grand and the praises of all of Europe'. But the unofficial epitaphs were less flattering: 'He is lewd and evil-minded and devours everything; his wife, children and all others large and small recite morning and night in their prayers "Lord in your bountiful goodness, deliver us from the Florentine".' There were heavily satirical accounts of Lully's arrival in heaven; on hearing a rumour that Orpheus played the lyre, he proposed to combine with him in creating an opera 'that will be worth money to

43. *François Couperin.*

us'. Lully admitted quite freely: 'I have worked usefully for the corruption of my century, but the French are no less deserving of the glory, because they have followed the composer's intentions.'

At Versailles a less flamboyant age was ushered in by a sequence of French defeats at Blenheim, Ramillies and Oudenarde. Three Dauphins had died in eleven months. Madame de Maintenon, now reinstated, was urging restraint and modesty; *la grand goût* of Louis XIV reverted to *divertissements* on the canals, with feasting, fireworks and anonymous jubilation, and eventually took comfort in more intimate concerts and, to his wife's approval, religious music. The grandeur of Versailles, with its 'symmetrical draughts', was exchanged for the greater comforts of the small château at Marly. The heroic style of Lebrun became less valued than the pastoral eloquence of Watteau, and although Louis never completely lost his taste for spectacle and ceremony, he no longer took any active part in the more grandiose forms of entertainment. The Marquis de Dangeau recorded sadly in his *Journal*: '14 October. . . . During the evening, the new opera of Destouches was performed. As the King rather likes the music of Destouches, it had been hoped that His Majesty would attend. But he has almost entirely renounced such performances.'

The scene was now set for the arrival of Lully's greatest successor, a man of totally different character, restrained in both life-style and music, reluctant to indulge in effect for its own sake. François Couperin (known as 'le Grand' to distinguish him from the other members of the musical dynasty) never wrote for the stage, remained aloof from public life, and distilled his greatest music in small forms. The four great collections of *Pièces de Clavecin*, and the *Concerts Royaux* were his offerings to the royal music parties held each Sunday. No longer the great band of *violons* but the most intimate chamber group — Duval on the violin, Alarius on the bass viol, Philidor and Dubois on oboe and bassoon, and Couperin himself at the harpsichord. It was a far cry indeed from the entry of the Sun King in the splendour of a Torelli stage set; *le Grand Goût* gave way to *le bon goût*, and 'the expression of thought, sentiment and passions' succeeded *le grand spectacle.*

IV

'ANNUS MIRABILIS'

On 23 February in the small North German town of Halle, Handel was born; Bach on 21 March in Eisenach, some eighty miles south; and on 26 October, in the feverish principality of Naples, Domenico Scarlatti. The year was 1685 — surely an '*annus mirabilis*' to produce the three great composers who together were to span the whole range of baroque music. From the elaborate confection of *opera seria* to the simplest of minuets for a beginner at the clavichord; from the most elementary flute sonata to the most exacting *partita* for unaccompanied violin; from *Salve Regina* to Lutheran chorale — there was no province of high baroque music that went unexplored by at least one member of the triumvirate.

Other than their year of birth, there is little to connect the three composers. The music of each, though based on the *lingua franca* of the early eighteenth century, is instantly distinguishable. So too, their attitudes to the established forms of patronage were individual and sometimes unorthodox. Between them they encountered the best and the worst that the courts of Europe could offer — from feasting and flattery to redundancy and imprisonment. Their reactions reveal unsuspected quirks of character, from the most foolhardy spirit of adventure to the bitterest sense of confinement.

Handel knew Scarlatti, but he never met Bach, though not for want of trying on the part of the latter. Hearing of Handel's first return visit to Halle, Bach set out from the court of Cöthen, a mere twenty miles away, only to find that Handel had just left for England. Handel, the restless cosmopolitan, was intolerant of confinement, be it the provincialism of Halle, the limitations of operatic life in Hamburg, the dogma of a church or even the preciosity of the Academia Poetico-Musicali of Cardinal Ottoboni.

Far from clerical in character, although cousin to the Pope, this leading patron of Rome's artistic community was remembered by de Brosses as being '*sans moeurs, sans crédit, débauché, ruiné, amateur des arts, grand musicien*'. Bored by the tediousness of a papal conclave, the story goes, he employed his private orchestra to entertain him outside his cell, much to the annoyance of some of his more orthodox colleagues. Wordly pleasures (he was credited with some sixty or seventy bastards) were clearly more inviting than thoughts of the hereafter. 'His Eminence keeps in his Pay, the best Musicians and Performers in Rome, and amongst others, the famous Archangelo Corelli, and young Paolucci, who is

44. Johann Sebastian Bach at the age of 61, painted by Gottlieb Haussmann. He is holding the music of a canon he wrote to qualify for the Society of the Musical Sciences.

reckoned the finest Voice in Europe; so that every Wednesday he has an excellent
Concert in his Palace, and we assisted there this very Day. We were there served
with iced and other delicate Liquors; and this is likewise the Custom when the
Cardinals or Roman Princess visit one another. But the greatest Inconveniency
in all these Concerts and Visits, is, that one is pestered with Swarms of trifling
little *Abbés*, who come thither on purpose to fill their Bellies with those Liquors,
and carry off the Crystal Bottles, with the Napkins into the Bargain.' As well as
arranging these concerts, his eminence also took an interest in the theatre,
mistakenly supplying both text and music for one entertainment, *Colombo*:
'Never was there subject more ridiculous or worse conceived. It concerned
Christopher Columbus who, in traversing the seas, falls passionately in love
with his own wife!'

It was in the artificial Arcadia of these 'academies', where poets and musicians,
rechristened 'nymphs and shepherds', disported themselves in 'huts and
pastures' (in fact, Roman palaces and formal gardens) that Handel the
cosmopolitan found himself at odds with the Italian style and temperament. 'It
was a customary thing with his eminence to have performances of Operas,
Oratorios, and such other grand compositions, as could from time to time be
procured. Handel was desired to furnish his quota; and there was always such a
greatness and superiority in the pieces composed by him, as rendered those of the
best masters comparatively little and insignificant. There was something in his
manner so very different from what the Italians had been used to, that those who
were seldom or never at a loss in performing any other Music, were frequently

45. *Engravings based on the
Howard portrait of Corelli were
included in most 18th century
English editions of his music.*

46. *Stage design by Filippo Juvarra for the theatre of Cardinal Ottoboni (probably for an opera by Domenico Scarlatti).*

puzzled how to execute his. Corelli himself complained of the difficulty he found in playing his Overtures. Several fruitless attempts Handel had one day made to instruct him in the manner of executing these spirited passages. Piqued at the tameness with which he still played them, he snatched the instrument out of his hand and played the passages himself. But Corelli, who was a person of great modesty and meekness, wanted no conviction of this sort; for he ingenuously declared that he did not understand them. When Handel appeared impatient, 'Ma, caro Sassone,' (said he), 'questa Musica é nel stylo Francese, di ch'io non m'intendo.'★

A French player would, of course, have found the same problems in performing music in the 'Italian Stile' since, at the very time when growing internationalism (typified by Handel), backed by intense activity from the commercial music publishers, was broadening the market for the 'foreign masters', national differences were exploited and encouraged by those at the centres of the Italian and French factions. Pamphleteering, propaganda and even physical violence were employed to establish the supremacy of French elegance and tranquility over Italian passion and agitation, or Parisian wit over Roman energy.

While German composers, especially Bach, did their best to reconcile these extremes, Handel was unique as a cosmopolitan, aloof from national affiliations,

★ 'But, my dear Saxon, this music is in the French style, which I do not understand.'

47. *George Frederick Handel; portrait attributed to R. Dandridge.*

striding from country to country with an independence of spirit that none of his contemporaries could match. At the opposite extreme was Scarlatti, the third of our miraculous trio, content to withdraw from the field of conflict and devote his energies to a single-minded pursuit of his own 'ingenious jesting with art'. Like Bach and Handel, his initial success was as a keyboard player: we even meet him in direct competition with Handel, at one of Cardinal Ottoboni's soirées, where it was decided that although honours might be equal in harpsichord-playing, on the organ 'Scarlatti himself declared the superiority of his antagonist'. Mattheson, our authority for this incident, distinguishes the competitors more precisely: 'Though no two persons ever arrived at such perfection on their respective instruments, yet it is remarkable that there was a total difference in their manner. The characteristic excellence of Scarlatti seems to have consisted in a certain elegance and delicacy of expression. Handel had an uncommon brilliancy and command of finger: but what distinguished him from all other players who possessed these same qualities, was that amazing fullness, force and energy, which he joined with them.'

But as Handel departed from Italy for the Hanoverian court in London, Scarlatti proceeded, via a post in the Vatican, to the entourage of the Portuguese court as music-master to the king's young brother Don Antonio, and the Infanta Maria Barbara, who in January 1729 left Lisbon and 'notwithstanding the deep snows, and much fatigu'd with the bad Weather, which had scarce ever ceas'd, from the Time they left' met, for the first time, her husband-to-be, Crown Prince Fernando of Spain.

The Infanta was no beauty: 'I had placed myself very conveniently yesterday to see the first meeting of the two families,' reported the British Ambassador, 'and I could not but observe, that the princess's figure, notwithstanding a profusion of gold and diamonds, really shocked the prince. He looked as if he thought he had been imposed upon. Her large mouth, thick lips, high cheek bones and small eyes, afforded him no agreeable prospect.' Since insanity and hypochondria had already overtaken the prince's father, the prospect was, indeed, far from ideal. Nevertheless, with 'a fine Consort of Music perform'd by the Musicians of both the King's Chapels', Scarlatti followed his royal pupil, and never left Spain for the rest of his life.

48. *Philip V of Spain and his family, by L. M. Van Loo; Ferdinand and Maria Barbara are on the left. The musicians are relegated to a distant tribune.*

Like those of Saul, the Spanish king's attacks of melancholia had only one cure, and that was music. He was of a dynasty of melomanes (his grandfather was Louis XIV) and, in a court that humoured his every whim (he dined at three in the morning, and went to bed at five) he was induced to moments of lucidity by the singing of the famous castrato Farinelli.

This great artist, probably the finest and certainly the most good-natured virtuoso there has ever been, had been for a time the rage of all Europe. 'In his voice, strength, sweetness and compass; in his stile, the tender, the graceful, and the rapid. He possessed such powers as never met before, or since, in any one human being; powers that were irresistible, and which must subdue every hearer; the learned and the ignorant, the friend and the foe' — so Burney claimed, who met him in retirement. Even the Emperor Charles VI maintained that everything about him 'was supernatural'. Yet after making a large fortune, mainly from English opera-lovers, he was persuaded to be taken into the service of the Spanish court on the discovery that the king's delirium was quieted by his performance. For a consideration of £2,000 a year, Burney reports: 'for the first ten years of his residence at the court of Spain, during the life of Philip, he sung every night to that monarch the same four airs, of which two were composed by Hasse . . . I forget the others, but one was a minuet which he used to vary at his pleasure.' The Orpheus of Europe, once greeted in the London opera with a cry of 'One God, one Farinelli', was reduced to the role of music-therapist, by Appointment.

49. *The arts at court: the painter Amiconi included himself, Metastasio (in clerical dress) and Farinelli together with Maria Barbara.*

50. *A lithograph said to be Domenico Scarlatti by Alfred Lemoine*, 1867.

However, the ambassador's description suggests a less than complete cure: 'Your Grace will smile when I inform you that the king himself imitates Farinelli, sometimes air after air, and sometimes after the music is over, and throws himself into such freaks and howlings that all possible means are taken to prevent people from being witness to his follies.' Eventually the disease, supplemented by what one historian discreetly terms '*trop de nourriture et d'exercise conjugal*' took its toll, and on 9 July 1746 his son Fernando was proclaimed king.

Once the fireworks, the bull-fights and the celebratory parades were forgotten, the new queen returned to her harpsichord and the ever-growing series of sonatas from the pen of 'Cavaliere Don Domenico' — by now Scarlatti had been knighted for his diligence and loyalty. But while Maria Barbara's quiet musical life centred on her music-master, the rest of the court delighted in the flamboyance of the operatic spectacles that Farinelli mounted in the theatre of the royal palace, Buen Retiro. Metastasio himself supplied most of the libretti — 'My Twin' as Farinelli referred to him, since they had made their debut together in the same production. The orchestra in their uniforms of scarlet and silver stood playing by the light of two hundred crystal chandeliers, the great salons were 'adorned and tiffed up in such a manner that it was *un Paradiso*', and as the last scene of the opera drew to a close, the back of the stage opened to reveal the long vista of the royal gardens illuminated by a display of fireworks. Small wonder that Farinelli, adding the role of impressario to that of virtuoso, minister, knight and ambassador, took all the attention.

But meanwhile what of Scarlatti? His work seems to have passed almost

51. *Sketch of a court concert by Zocchi, where performers outnumber audience by three to one. The position of the horns is a reminder of their alternative use in the hunting-field.*

unnoticed, except by the queen, and of all his five-hundred and fifty-one sonatas for the harpsichord, only thirty were actually printed during his lifetime. These were the set of *Essercizi per Gravicembalo*, elaborately engraved by Fortier (although by mistake he reversed the picture of the harpsichord on the title-page!): '*Curarum Levamen*' would seem the only appropriate motto to issue from the troubled Bourbon household. But it was London, rather than Madrid, that saw the publication of this magnificent edition — England was almost the only place outside the Spanish court to recognize the merits of Scarlatti's compositions, apart from his performance of them, during his lifetime. The 'Scarlatti Sect' included Viscount Fitzwilliam, whose fine collection of music still exists in the Cambridge museum that he founded; Charles Burney, who 'kept Scarlatti's best lessons in constant practice'; Dr Worgan; Thomas Roseingrave, who had not been able to touch the harpsichord for a month after first hearing Scarlatti play in Italy; the two Wesley brothers, and, of course, Mr Handel.

Since parting from Scarlatti in Arcadia, Handel had learned to 'manage' patronage better than any of his contemporaries. It is his career, rather than Mozart's or Beethoven's, that marks the end of the baroque notion of the composer-as-servant and the dawning of the individual voice. The musician was the equal of the monarch. The building of the pedestal had begun. With an appointment as Kapellmeister to the Elector of Hanover safely in his pocket,

Handel left for the gold-mine of London, and there received patronage on his own terms. First in the newly finished Burlington House (standing in fields that few would guess existed when visiting the Royal Academy today), where the seventeen-year-old earl entertained the composer — under the watchful eye of his mother. Handel, fortunately, was very 'regular and uniform in his habits'.

After Burlington House came Canons, 'the most magnificent palace in England' according to Defoe. James Brydges (Lord Chandos) had mysteriously amassed a fortune while Paymaster-General for Marlborough's wars; £230,000 of it he spent on marble staircases, Italian paintings, a private chapel (which still stands in Edgware), and the maintenance of a complete orchestra, under the direction of Dr Pepusch. Not everyone was impressed by this ostentation. Pope objected both to the chapel and its music:

> And now the Chapel's silver bell you hear,
> That summons you to all the Pride of Pray'r:
> Light quirks of Music, broken and uneven,
> Make the soul dance upon a Jig to Heaven.

And he said of the mansion:

> Lo, what huge heaps of littleness around!
> The whole, a labour'd Quarry above ground.

For the owner, however, there were only two blots on this Paradise: the

52. *A less flattering portrayal of an Italian concert party by Gaspare Traversi.*

highwaymen who frequented the Edgware Road and the tedium of Pepusch. The earl had to endure the first, but solved the second by firing the good doctor and appointing Handel in his place.

At last a court to compare with continental establishments! Handel responded with the Chandos Anthems, first performed in the tiny chapel decorated by Grinling Gibbons, the serenata *Acis and Galatea*, a pastoral entertainment apt for this rural setting, and his first venture into oratorio, *Esther.* But he never could equate himself with the liveried servants; he would commute between Canons and the duke's town house in Albémarle Street, from where he conducted his business with the Opera, invested his profits, unhappily, in the South Sea Bubble, and re-established his favour with the new king — none other than the Elector he had abandoned in Hanover — now George I.

Tales of an estrangement between the two were invented to suit a romantic concept of court etiquette; and, despite legend, the composition of the *Water Music* never implied a cringing plea for reconciliation. It is, nevertheless, an endearing example of the English not *quite* achieving the natural grandeur that accompanied the aquatic parties on the canals of Versailles, or the Spanish

53. *Dido and Aeneas. A design by Sir James Thornhill, probably for Canons.*

expeditions on the Tagus; Chelsea was hardly Cytherea, and the banqueting arrangements have that air of 'teas will be available'.

About eight in the evening the King repaired to His barge into which were admitted the Duchess of Bolton, Countess Godolphin, Mad. de Kilmanseck, Mrs Were and the Earl of Orkney, the Gentleman of the Bedchamber in Waiting. Next to the King's barge was that of the musicians, about 50 in number, who played on all kinds of instruments, to wit trumpets, horns, hautboys, bassoons, German flutes, French flutes, violins and basses; but there were no singers. The music had been composed specially by the famous Handel, a native of Halle, and His Majesty's principal Court Composer. His Majesty approved of it so greatly that he caused it to be repeated three times in all, although each performance lasted an hour — namely twice before and once after supper. The [weather in the] evening was all that could be desired for the festivity, the number of barges and above all of boats filled with people desirous of hearing was beyond counting. In order to make this entertainment the more exquisite, Mad. de Kilmanseck had arranged a choice supper in the late Lord Ranelagh's villa at Chelsea on the river, where the King went at one in the morning. He left at three o'clock and returned to St James's about half past four. The concert cost Baron Kilmanseck £150 for the musicians alone.

The contrast between that royal picnic and activities in the small German court of Weimar makes sobering reading; fifty musicians, so casually assembled for the evening's entertainment against less than fifteen on regular pay in the Castle Kapelle of the Prince of Saxe-Weimar (and six of these were ceremonial trumpeters). The £150 that the baron grudgingly paid out (his wife was the king's mistress) was real extravagance beside the 250 thalers allowed *per year* to Konzertmeister Bach — supplemented though it was with an allowance of coal and firewood. While Handel retired to the glamour of Canons, Bach's situation that same year was described curtly in the Weimar accounts: 'On 6 November, the quondam Konzertmeister and organist Bach was confined to the County Judge's place of detention for too stubbornly forcing the issue of his dismissal and finally on 2 December was freed from arrest with notice of his unfavourable discharge.'

Sadly, Bach had neither the quiet dedication of Scarlatti to his queen, nor the opportunist charm of Handel over his princes. Ten years of Weimar had tried his patience; the next six were spent in the more friendly atmosphere of Cöthen, with a music-loving prince and a salary increase of 150 thalers. Bach's good fortune ended when the prince married a woman with no interest in his art: the composer described her resignedly as 'an *amusa*'. The prince, a staunch Calvinist, had no time for elaborate church music, and during these years Bach composed the greater part of all his secular instrumental music: the English and

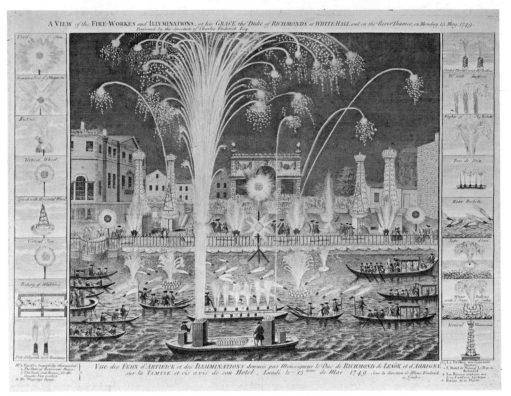

VUE des FEUX d'ARTIFICE et des ILLUMINATIONS données par Monseigneur le Duc de RICHMOND de LENOX et d'AUBIGNY
sur la TAMISE et vis à vis de son Hotel, Lundi le 15.ème de Mai 1749. Sous la direction de Monsr Charles Frederick

54. *A firework display on the Thames*, 15 *May* 1749, *promoted by the Duke of Richmond in emulation of the Royal Fireworks. The king's barge can be seen at the right.*

French Suites, the solo violin and cello music, the violin concertos. . . . The small band of regular players was supplemented by any other musicians who could be found — cooks, stewards, gardeners were all called in. (Rather similarly, we find at Canons a second violinist who combined work as a valet with inventing a new form of fire engine; also one who 'shaves very well & hath an excellent hand on the violin. . .')

Bach's more tedious duties of having to follow his prince around on tour gave him the opportunity of making useful acquaintances. A trip to the spa of Karlsbad brought him into contact with the Margrave of Brandenburg, and, quick to see the possibility of a change of job, Bach enthusiastically prepared a set of sample concertos and a letter of dedication (written in French that is surely too good to be Bach's own work):

To His Royal Highness My Lord Christian Louis Elector of Brandenburg etc., etc., etc.

YOUR ROYAL HIGHNESS,

As I had a couple of years ago the pleasure of appearing before Your Royal Highness, by virtue of Your Highness' commands, and as I notice then that Your Highness took some pleasure in the insignificant talents which Heaven has given me for Music, and as in taking leave of Your Royal Highness, Your Highness deigned to honour me with the command to send Your Highness some pieces of my Composition: I have then in accordance with Your Highness's most gracious orders taken the liberty of rendering my most humble duty to Your Royal Highness with the present Concertos, which I have adapted to several instruments; begging Your Highness most humbly not to judge their imperfection with the rigour of the fine and delicate taste which the whole world knows Your Highness has for musical pieces; but rather to infer from them in benign Consideration the profound respect and the most humble obedience which I try to show Your Highness therewith. For the rest, Sire, I beg Your Royal Highness very humbly to have the goodness to continue Your Highness' gracious favour toward me, and to be assured that nothing is so close to my heart as the wish that I may be employed on occasions more worthy of Your Royal Highness and of Your Highness' service — I, who without an equal in zeal am, Sire, Your Royal Highness' most humble and obedient servant

JEAN SEBASTIEN BACH

Cöthen, 24 March 1721

His lack of success is well known. The Brandenburg Concertos and a complete set of parts, in Bach's fair copy, lay on the shelves of the Margrave's library; they were unopened when musicologists discovered them long after Bach's death. To an advanced art lover of that time, Bach's wry description of his talents as 'insignificant' probably seemed only too true; the great men were Telemann, Graupner, Fischer, Mattheson. And Bach, ever hopeful of some preferment, never succeeded in rising above a mediocre court post. Ironically, his visit to Frederick the Great was not even in a professional capacity — it was as a father, simply visiting one of his sons fortunate enough to be employed by 'the greatest monarch in Europe'.

V

SANS SOUCI

'Gentlemen, Old Bach has arrived!' It was almost seven o'clock, and the musicians were already assembling for the evening concert. King Frederick put away his flute, the performance was adjourned and Bach was shown round the musical novelties of the royal palace. First amongst them were the new 'fortepianos' that Silbermann was producing; Frederick owned no fewer than fifteen of them (one can still be seen standing beneath the great chandelier in the music room of the Stadtschloss) and he was anxious to know what Bach, the great keyboard virtuoso, would think of them. Frederick was also very curious to hear a display of Bach's fabled powers of improvisation, and, leading him to one of the fortepianos, he 'condescended to play, in person and without any preparation, a theme to be executed by Kapellmeister Bach in a fugue. This was done so happily by the aforementioned Kappelmeister that not only His Majesty was pleased to show his satisfaction thereat, but also all those present were seized with astonishment. Mr Bach has found the subject propounded to him so exceedingly beautiful that he intends to set it down on paper in a regular fugue and have it engraved on copper.'

In fact, Bach did much more than that. Two months after this visit Frederick received *A Musical Offering*, engraved and finely bound and containing the three-part Ricercare. In style it is less concentrated than much of Bach's fugal writing, the episodes are determinedly 'modern' and the inflections almost rococo; all of which suggest it may indeed be a tidied up version of Bach's improvisation. If so, it is the only authentic piano piece by Bach! He was obviously intrigued by the king's theme:

It is, flatteringly enough, very like the one Bach himself chose for the *Art of Fugue* two years later, and it proved so amenable to contrapuntal tricks that Bach included in the same offering a set of six canons and a *fuga canonica*. He even attached slightly heavy-handed Latin compliments to some of these; a canon in augmentation was inscribed *Notulis cresentibus crescat Fortuna Regis* ('As the little notes increase, so may the Fortune of the King'), and another, in ascending modulation, hoped that 'as the modulations rise, so may the King's Glory'. Amenable though he was to flattery, there is no evidence that the king ever played Bach's music — not even the trio sonata that arrived as a second instalment of the gift, specially scored to include the flute, and with a fulsome dedication declaring the piece to be written 'with the single and laudable desire to exalt, though in a minor sphere, the fame of a potentate whose greatness in the realm of music no less than in the arts of war and peace, is acclaimed and admired by all'.

Frederick's reputation in music was certainly deserved; enlightened despotism required a personal involvement in the arts and letters, which the king organized with the same enthusiasm as he devoted to a military campaign. He demanded from his musicians the same precision as he demanded from his regiments. 'Those who seek for art, true and clear philosophy, and wit should come here,' wrote Princess Elizabeth from Rheinsberg. 'They will find everything in a state of perfection, as our master is in control of it all. I have never seen anyone work as hard as he does: from six in the morning until one o'clock he works at reading, philosophy and all the other noble studies. Dinner lasts from half-past one until three o'clock. After that we drink coffee until four and then he gets down to work again till seven in the evening. Next music begins and lasts till nine o'clock. Then he writes, comes to play cards, and we generally sup at half-past ten or eleven. . . . I can truthfully say that he is the greatest prince of our time.'

The flute was Frederick's constant consolation; he played to relax himself before cabinet meetings, pacing up and down his room. He took it on campaign with him, together with an ingenious collapsible harpsichord that folded into three sections for travelling. His performances in the royal music room were

55. *Frederick the Great, by J. G. Ziesenis.*

regular evening occurrences, to which only select audiences were admitted. Charles Burney wrote:

I was carried to one of the interior apartments of the palace, in which the gentlemen of the king's band were waiting for his commands. This apartment was contiguous to the concert-room, where I could distinctly hear his majesty practising *Solfeggi* on the flute, and exercising himself in difficult passages, previous to his calling in the band. Here I met with M. Benda, who was so obliging as to introduce me to M. Quantz.

The concert began by a German flute concerto, in which his majesty executed the solo parts with great precision; his *embouchure* was clear and even, his finger brilliant, and his taste pure and simple. I was much pleased, and even surprised with the neatness of his execution in the *allegros*, as well as by his expression and feeling in the *adagio*; in short, his performance surpassed, in many particulars, any thing I had ever heard among *Dilettanti*, or even professors. His majesty played three long and difficult concertos successively, and all with equal perfection.

M. Quantz bore no other part in the performance of the concertos of to-night than to give the time with the motion of his hand, at the beginning of each movement, except now and then to cry out *bravo!* to his royal scholar, at the end of the solo parts and closes; which seems to be a privilege allowed to no other musician of the band. The cadences which his majesty made, were good, but very long and studied. It is easy to discover that these concertos were composed at a time when he did not so frequently require an opportunity of breathing as at present; for in some of the divisions, which were very long and difficult, as well as in the closes, he was obliged to take his breath, contrary to rule, before the passages were finished.

With the exception of that one small criticism, Burney's opinion of the king's ability as a performer was much more enthusiastic than flattery would have demanded, though one takes it that the resident composers would never have been so tactless as to write a solo passage beyond the king's capabilities. Voltaire, who candidly admitted that he had, as he put it, 'never perceived the virtue of semi-quavers', nevertheless managed to 'squeeze a facile tear as the King completed some adagio of his own composition'.

Frederick's activities were not limited to playing. The whole foundation of Berlin's musical life during the mid-eighteenth century rested upon his likes and dislikes, as Burney was quick to understand: 'From the year of 1742, when the King of Prussia fixed the musical activities of his opera and court, so many eminent musicians were engaged in his service, that Berlin seems to have given the law to the rest of Germany . . .' The law, however, as far as Frederick's taste went, was simple enough: '*La musique française ne vaut rien. La France pour*

56. '*Flute Concerto at Sans Souci*' *by Adolf von Menzel. C. P. E. Bach is at the harpsichord, and Quantz listens discreetly at the extreme right.*

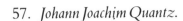
57. *Johann Joachim Quantz.*

JOHANN IOACHIM QUANZ

littérature, l'Italie pour la musique.' Italianate opera therefore headed the list, wherever possible composed by Graun or Hasse, and performed by singers and dancers of his own choosing in the opera house he had had specially designed. In instrumental music, the only things he really cared for had prominent parts for solo flute, and were composed either by himself, or Quantz.

Quantz held a unique position in Frederick's household — with a salary of 2,000 thalers a year, he was more highly paid than any other windplayer of the time. On top of this there were supplements at the rate of a hundred ducats for every new concerto he produced, twenty-five for every new sonata, and a hundred for every flute that was built for the king under his supervision. As he wrote no less than 153 sonatas and 296 concertos during his thirty-two years in Berlin, he can hardly have complained of his position. His association with the king had started while Frederick was still Crown Prince. Quantz visited the palace in secret twice a week to give him flute lessons (and was once unceremoniously bundled into a cupboard when Frederick's monstrous father

Wilhelm appeared unannounced). It was Quantz who drilled into Frederick the three attributes that he, and all Berlin, considered music should display: 'a singable and interesting melody, deep feeling and, most important of all, "correctness".'

It was this last quality that produced the inevitable petrification of Frederick's, and Berlin's, taste at this period, rather than the king's capacity as a performer or the restrictions of the royal band. The king was rather of Voltaire's view that all contrapuntal music fell under the heading of plain-chant. On the other hand, he found in Haydn's symphonies nothing but 'a din to flay the ears' — so the scope for development was severely restricted. His own works, though, met Quantz's requirements to perfection. There seems to be no evidence at all for doubting that he did write the works attributed to him — there are autograph versions available, with mistakes corrected in the king's own hand. What is amazing is that he found any time in which to compose at all, considering the average day of a ruling monarch. Clearly he was best at easy melodic thinking, but the harmonies are, at least, pleasantly progressive. It is the sentimental Frederick, the man who wept when reading scenes from Racine, or when moved by the loyalty of his soldiers, who is most indicative of the intense emotionalism behind the very rational front of Berlin thinking; and, in such an atmosphere, it is easy to believe Reichardt's claim that when the king played one of his own adagios, 'his audience seldom listened without tears'.

He allowed no emotionalism to disrupt the organization of his music, however; and there is little indication of warmth in the way he sympathized with his sister Wilhelmina over her problems: 'I am sorry to hear, my dear sister, that a revolt has taken place among your musicians. This race of creatures is very difficult to govern; reigning over a group of musicians requires more care than the conduct of affairs of state . . . I am waiting for some new sedition among my own children of Euterpe.'

No campaign in the whole of Frederick's military career was organized with more despotic precision than the building of the new opera house. It was his first work as king. He had come to the throne in May, and by early June Graun had been despatched to Italy to hire singers with instructions that 2,000 thalers was the maximum fee he could offer to any one person. His envoy in Paris was instructed to hire suitable ballet dancers, and shortly afterwards Voltaire himself was pressed into action in the French capital with demands that he engage a comedian and a troupe of actors. Most elaborate of all were the manoeuvres to find a suitable site on which to erect the longest, widest and most expensively equipped theatre in the world. Plans had already been drawn up by Frederick's architect friend Knobelsdorf, and a site was eventually cleared in the Linden-Allee by demolishing a fort. The present Deutsche Staatsoper occupies the same site, and is the third copy of the original to be built there. Just before its

58. *The Royal Opera House in* 1773; coloured engraving by J. G. Rosenberg.

opening performance in 1955 an order came that the inscription across the front, FREDERICUS REX APOLLONI ET MUSIC, should be removed; the conductor, Erich Kleiber, walked out.

The building of Frederick's masterpiece (with the above motto inscribed) was controlled from a distance by the king on campaign in Silesia, and inevitably, was incomplete when the first performance took place. The carefully selected audience had to pick their way through the builders' rubble towards the brilliantly lit foyer. However, the architect's published description contained an extensive description of its very advanced features, many of which stemmed from the king's active and practical mind.

Its long façade of Corinthian columns enabled no less than a hundred carriages to draw up around it; to one side of the building was what must then have been the world's finest car-park, with room for a thousand vehicles. The staircases were so wide that sedan chairs could be carried up to the fourth tier of boxes, and the whole auditorium was lit (at an expense of 2,770 thalers a night!) by three enormous chandeliers.

In view of the fire hazard, the prudent Knobelsdorf had included in his scheme a canal that ran under the theatre and 'from which, by means of two pumps, great quantities of water can be brought into reservoirs just below the roof.

Through a system of pipes, this water can not only be used in decorative cascades and jets, but can be made to saturate the whole theatre in case of fire'.

The acoustic, everyone admitted, was most favourable. 'Even when a singer is standing backstage, not only can his most delicate tones be heard equally well in the farthest balcony and on the main floor, but he can also hear the effect he produces and judge his own performance with exactness. Few theatres offer such advantages to singers.' Spitta recounted the story of Bach being taken to see the new opera house and detecting everything about its acoustic without hearing a note of music in it: 'He also pointed out to his companions in the dining-room attached to the opera-house, an acoustic phenomenon which, as he supposed, the architect had probably not intended to produce. The form of the arches betrayed the secret to him. When a speaker stood in one corner of the gallery of the hall — which was longer than square — whispered against the wall, another person, standing in the corner diagonally opposite, with his face to the wall, could hear what was said though no one else could. Bach detected this at a glance, and experiment proved him to be right.'

Most impressive of all was the machinery to convert the theatre into a dance hall while the court was dining in this adjacent room after the performance. The whole floor of the theatre, where the audience had stood during the performance, rose on pneumatic jacks to the height of the stage: the scenery and machines disappeared behind Corinthian columns, and marble nymphs appeared in niches with water cascading from their urns. The banquet completed, Frederick would return to the ballroom to lead off the first minuet, accompanied by his band of twenty-four oboes (possibly in the manner of Louis XIV's *Vingt-quatre Violons*).

The king had a hand in every aspect of the theatre: he coached singers personally, decided on scenery and costumes, sacked performers on impulse, rewrote or changed both music and libretto as he liked, and persistently hurled into prison mutinous ballet dancers or rebellious sopranos who got in his way. He had no time for local singers ('A German singer? I should as soon expect to receive pleasure from the neighing of my horse!'), yet the foreigners gave continuous trouble and cost a small fortune: Astrua got 6,000 thalers a year, Salimbeni 4,000, and Porporino, who had the devotion to declare that his voice was 'for God and the King of Prussia only', 2,000. C. P. E. Bach, by contrast, was engaged at a mere three *hundred*.

For one of the most successful operas by Graun, *Montezuma*, Frederick himself wrote the libretto, and acquitted himself very creditably. He confessed himself tired of the stock characters of *opera seria*, and with the tediousness of *da capo* arias. In *Montezuma* he had a plot close to his heart — it is set in Mexico, where Cortez is determined to convert the natives at any price. Frederick, a rationalist and anti-Christian, made of Montezuma a noble resister who would rather die than accept beliefs that were unnatural to him. 'You know, of course,' he wrote to a friend, 'that I shall be on the side of Montezuma, that Cortez will be the tyrant, and that as a result a few telling remarks can be made, even in music, against the barbarousness of the Christian religion.'

He felt himself an innovator also in deterring Graun from the usual *da capo* form by supplying texts with sections of contrasting emotion. 'Repeats', he said, 'are not worthwhile unless a singer really knows how to vary the music; but in any case, I consider it an abuse to repeat the same thing four times.'

The power wielded by Graun in the opera and Quantz at court was obviously resented by the other employees of Frederick, and much eloquent satire circulated, no doubt under cover.

'Which', they asked, 'is the most fearsome animal in the Prussian monarchy? It is Madame Quantz's lap-dog. He is so terrifying that Madame Quantz quails before him; Herr Quantz, in turn is afraid of Madame Quantz, and the greatest of all monarchs fears Herr Quantz!'

The story came from Carl Philip Emmanuel Bach, who, of all the resident musicians, had good reason to feel his talents wasted on the court duties that he was compelled to fulfill as official accompanist to the king — not the easiest of tasks by all accounts. The king's sense of rhythm was none too good, and passages that he couldn't manage at speed he would just play slower. When some sycophantic courtier remarked of the king's performance 'Ah, what rhythm', Carl Philip was heard to murmur: 'Ah, but what rhythms.' The greatest disappointment for him was that the king showed no interest at all in his compositions.

Even allowing for hindsight, it does seem to have been sheer blindness on Frederick's part to have promoted the stereotyped work of Quantz and given so little encouragement to the much wilder and more fascinating products of C. P. E. Bach. But Bach certainly knew himself to follow the more startling line of thought of the enlightened philosophers and literary men that made up his society in Berlin, and despite his regard for the 'learned style' of his father, Carl Philip's compositions moved away from the pedantry of counterpoint towards the polish of the galant style. From the literary *Sturm und Drang* movement around him he absorbed something to add to the elegance of the galant. The continual tension in his music is the struggle to achieve that fusion of passion and principle which became the definition of classicism, and it reveals in his works a streak of passionate romanticism. His musical aesthetic, though discussed in rational terms, was far from cold: 'A musician', he says, 'cannot move others unless he too is moved. He must of necessity feel all of the effect that he hopes to arouse in his audience.' Even Carl Philip's manner of playing betrayed this very personal emotion — although it found little sympathy at court. Burney described a vivid evening he later spent at Bach's house: 'After dinner, which

59. *Carl Philip Emanuel Bach.*

was elegantly served and cheerfully eaten, I prevailed upon him to sit down to a clavichord and he played with little intermission till near eleven o'clock at night. During that time he grew so animated and possessed that he not only played but looked like one inspired. His eyes were fixed, his underlip fell, and drops of effervescence distilled from his countenance.'

Almost all Carl Philip's ideas on expression in music were borne out in the treatises written by the prolific theorists of Frederick's Berlin. 'Musical controversies in Berlin', said the indispensable Burney, 'have been carried on with more heat and animosity than elsewhere; indeed there are more critics and theorists in this city than practitioners, which has not, perhaps, either refined the taste or fed the fancy of the performers.' Marpurg, for instance, expressed exactly the practical application of *Empfindsamkeit* — the expressive power and sensibility upon which Carl Philip's music depends for a stylish performance. He also amplified the then current feeling that great art is an imitation of Nature, applying the principles of Enlightenment to the passions. Just as the Ency-clopaedists had examined and explained the physical world, so the musician, it was felt, could illuminate the passions and sensibilities. Probably for the first time in musical history, the performer could be viewed as a creature of individual emotions, to be judged by the degree to which he could identify himself with the changing moods of the work of art.

Despite his devotion to the principles of Enlightenment, it does seem that Frederick the Great had allied himself to the most static elements in his court music, 'the one languid', so Burney summed it up, 'and the other frequently common and insipid — and yet their names are religion at Berlin, and more sworn by than Luther or Calvin; for though a universal toleration prevails here, as to different sects of Christians, yet, in music, whoever dares to profess any other tenets than those of Graun and Quantz is sure to be persecuted. So that music is truly stationary in this country, his majesty allowing no more liberty in that, than he does in civil matters of government: not contented with being sole monarch of the lives, fortunes, and business of his subjects, he even prescribes rules to their most innocent pleasures.'

60. *Lady Mary Wortley Montagu in oriental costume.*

VI
AN ARMY OF
GENERALS

It is curious how rarely travellers' tales agree. What for one is charming, agreeable and admirably furnished is for another boorish, uncultivated and universally disagreeable. To one traveller ruins represent the most eloquent memorial to antiquity, to the other they are no more than a heap of decaying rubble. The eighteenth century exponents of the Grand Tour were no exception, and it is well to remind ourselves of their varied responses before taking their comments about music too readily on trust. Their very methods of travel occasioned quite dissimilar reactions. Lady Mary Wortley Montagu, for example, took the traditional route down the Rhine towards Vienna in 'one of those little vessels, that they very properly call wooden houses, having in them all the conveniences of a palace, stoves in the chambers, kitchens, etc. They are rowed by twelve men each, and move with such incredible swiftness that in the same day you have the pleasure of a vast variety of prospects.' But the prospects were bleak for the persistent Dr Burney when he tried river travel:

It was six o'clock in the evening, when I arrived at the waterside; I was much disturbed at seeing the boat, in which I was to perform the voyage; it was long, narrow, and quite open at the top. There was straw to lie on, but nothing to cover me or my baggage in case of rain; at this time, indeed, the weather was hot, and I nestled into my straw, accommodating myself to my circumstances as well as I could. The boat moved so very slow that it frequently seemed to stand still. The weather as yet continued calm, but as we proceeded lower down the river, through an amazingly wild and rocky country, there were frequent waterfalls that made a violent noise, and seemed very likely to overset our little boat; about midnight it grew totally dark, and began to rain: I protected my head as well as I was able, with a *parapluye*, or small umbrella, but was very wet elsewhere. The rain continued till day-break, after which, the wind got up, and became quite furious, just in our teeth; in this kind of hurricane, the boat could make no way. Distress on distress! the *parapluye*, my only defence, was forced from my hands, in a violent gust of wind, and blown into the river, where it instantly sunk; and we tried in vain, a considerable time, to fish it up: I was now wet, cold, hungry, and totally helpless . . .

61. *A caricature of London's Sunday Concerts, with Dr Burney (bottom right) unable to refrain from gossip even during the performance. The players include such celebrities as Cervetto, the cellist (famous for his nose and longevity) and the oboeist Fischer, playing behind the harpsichord.*

62. *Two views of Mannheim; the Theatre Square and the Palace Gardens,* c.1780.

Despite the tribulations of travel, all travellers on this Rhine route were unanimously ecstatic in their praise of one city — the Elector Palatine's newly designed capital of Mannheim. 'One of the most handsome little towns of Europe,' decided William Beckford: 'Numbers of well-dressed people were amusing themselves with music and fireworks in the squares and open spaces. Other groups appeared conversing in circles before their doors, and enjoying the serenity of the evening. Almost every window bloomed with carnations; and we could hardly cross a street without hearing a German flute.' Burney also admired the neatness of the town, with its oval plan, and streets running in straight lines from one end to the other — a novel design in town planning for that time.

Only a few years earlier the elector had decided to move his seat of government from the ruined castle of Heidelberg to the modernized city of Mannheim some thirteen miles away. The elector's hospitality was prodigious; in the village of Schwetzingen, halfway between Mannheim and Heidelberg, where he kept a summer palace, the entourage he entertained amounted to 'fifteen hundred persons, who are all lodged in this little village, at his expense'. All visitors were welcome and reported home in fulsome prose — all except one. Boswell, travelling a few years before Burney made his tour, did not attempt to conceal his disappointment. The elector, he reported, was 'very high and mighty', displaying a wife 'much painted' and a marked lack of the hospitality that 'Baron Boswell' felt to be his due. 'I have not been asked once. . . . What an inhospitable dog! I have been obliged to dine at an ordinary, amongst fellows of all sorts and sizes. It was one of the best tables in town, but the company disgusted me sadly. O British, take warning from me and shun the dominions of the Elector Palatine.' But even the snobbery of a Boswell could not deny that one thing about the court was 'magnificent': its music.

The building of the new palace, designed in the manner of Versailles, was

63. *Burney as Doctor of Music, painted by his friend Reynolds; one copy was sent to Padre Martini in Bologna, and another to Oxford to celebrate his doctorate.*

followed by the construction of an impressive new opera house, capable of holding an audience of five thousand. Performances began in November and continued twice weekly until Shrove Tuesday. Not only the opera house, but also its setting was calculated to impress. 'The going out from the opera at Schwetzingen, during summer, into the electoral gardens, which, in the French style, are extremely beautiful, affords one of the gayest and most splendid sights imaginable; the country here is flat, and naked, and therefore would be less favourable to the free and open manner of laying out grounds in English horticulture, than to that which has been adopted. The orangery is larger than that at Versailles, and perhaps than any other in Europe', wrote Burney.

He, unlike his fellow travellers, was almost the only person to apply a critical eye to the financing of this paradise. Throughout his commentaries on the *Present State of Music in Europe* we find continual reminders of the social injustices which lay behind the façade of prodigality. In Dresden he noted that even the horses had been allowed no corn, 'nor the soldiers powder for their hair' for three years, and, though remarking on the magnificence of the court at Mannheim, he added that 'the palaces and offices extend over almost the town; and one half of the inhabitants, who are in office, prey on the other, who seem to be in the utmost indigence'. The cost of the wax candles used for lighting the opera house for a single performance came to over £40, and the expense of mounting a new production approached £4,000.

When one remembers that the operas commissioned for this theatre included *Lucio Silla* from J. C. Bach and *La Clemenza di Tito* from Mozart, and were provided with some of Europe's most elaborate sets by the brothers Bibiena, the cost of the mere lighting dwindles into insignificance. The opening opera was composed by J. C. Bach, who 'was daily expected here from London, when I was in Mannheim'. *Temistocle* was presented on 5 November, at a gala occasion, given before an audience whose names read rather like a page from the *Almanach de Gotha*:

At four in the afternoon a procession was formed in the ante-room of the Electress's apartments in the left wing of the Schloss, whence, under the blare of trumpets, their Electoral Serenities were conducted to a box in the middle of the first tier. Persons of distinction graced the occasion and made their compliments; the young Margraves of Baden, with their suites; the Crown Prince and Princess of Hessen-Cassel; the Prince and Princess of Nassau-Weilburg; the Countess of Neipperg; and the three Princes Radziwill. Several foreign ladies of rank received places formerly reserved for the Jesuits, while other parts of the huge building were occupied by such a concourse of visitors that the townspeople, usually admitted to the parterre, were unable to gain admission.

Only the singers seem to have given cause for complaint — possibly there were greater attractions in operatic productions elsewhere, or possibly they were

64. *Backdrop for an unknown opera by Giuseppe Galli da Bibiena.*

allowed to continue beyond retirement age. Mozart, on his first visit to the town, when he was twenty-one and job-hunting, wrote to his father: 'Now for the opera, but quite briefly. Holzbauer's music is very beautiful. The poetry doesn't deserve such music. What surprises me most of all is that a man as old as Holzbauer should still possess so much spirit; for you can't imagine what fire there is in that music. The *prima donna* was Mme Elizabeth Wendling. She is always indisposed and, what is more, the opera was not written for her, but for a certain Danzi, who is at present in England; consequently it is not suited to her voice, but is too high for her. On one occasion Raaff sang four arias, about 450 bars in all, in such fashion as to call forth the remark that his voice was the strongest reason why he sang so badly. Anyone who hears him begin an aria without at once reminding himself that it is Raaff, the once famous tenor, who is singing, is bound to burst out laughing.'

Perhaps the example of the neighbouring Duke of Württemberg, who had just bankrupted his entire principality to provide operatic sensations, exercised a

65. *Maximilian III, Elector of Bavaria playing the bass-viol. His son Karl Theodore succeeded him in 1777, and left Mannheim.*

66. *Karl Theodore as Elector of Bavaria.*

little restraining influence on Karl Theodore. Though equally hedonistic, he was less exclusive in his tastes, and more liberal in his encouragement to a new-found style, and to the continual experimentation that he supported. 'Music awoke the elector in the morning,' wrote the critic Daniel Schubart; 'it accompanied him at the hunt; he prayed with it at church; it lulled him to sleep at night, and it is to be hoped that at the end it greeted this truly good prince at the gates of heaven.' For many of the expatriate musicians who found so accommodating a home in Mannheim, it must have already seemed like heaven.

But of even greater repute than the Mannheim opera was its orchestra, which moved Burney to raptures:

I found the Mannheim Orchestra to be indeed all that its fame had made me expect: power will naturally arise from a great number of hands; but the judicious use of this power, on all occasions, must be the consequence of good discipline, indeed there are more solo players, and composers in this than perhaps in any other orchestra in Europe; it is an army of generals, equally fit to plan a battle, as to fight it.

It was here that Stamitz first surpassed the bounds of common opera overtures, which had hitherto only served in the theatre as a kind of court cryer, with an 'O Yes!' in order to awaken attention, and bespeak silence, at the entrance of the singers. Since the discovery which the genius of Stamitz first made every effect has been tried which such an aggregate of sound can produce;

it was here that the *Crescendo* and *Diminuendo* had birth; and the *Piano*, which was before chiefly used as an echo, with which it was generally synonomous, as well as the *Forte*, were found to be musical *colours* which had their *shades*, as much as red or blue in painting.

Burney is wrong to claim precedence in those effects for the Mannheim orchestra. We know from Reichardt's *Letters* that the power of a long crescendo had already been noted with some amusement in Italy: 'When Jomelli caused this to be heard in Rome for the first time, the audience gradually rose from their seats with the crescendo and did not breathe again until the diminuendo, when they first observed that they were out of breath. This last effect,' he added, 'I have observed myself in Mannheim!' The elector's 'army of generals' were certainly the first orchestra to indulge in this device as a regular ingredient of their style, although it was only one of many techniques which became associated with them.

If nicknames indicate widespread popularity, their application to these tricks is a measure of the influence they had on classical composers. There was the 'Mannheim sigh', which ends so many affecting slow movements by Haydn and Mozart; the long crescendo became known as the 'Mannheim steamroller;'; interpolated trills and turns from the woodwind were 'Mannheim birdies'; and,

67. *Outdoor concert at Schloss Ismaning.*

most dramatic of all, was the 'Mannheim skyrocket'. This energetic rising arpeggio, heard at the start of Beethoven's first piano sonata, the last movement of Mozart's G minor Symphony (no. 40), and innumerable other places was a seminal idea of classical thought.

The chief architect of these wonders was neither a nobleman, nor even German, but an expatriate Bohemian, Johann Stamitz, whom Karl Theodore had first met as a violinist playing at the coronation of the Emperor Charles VII at Frankfurt in 1741. Appointed to the new orchestra, he became Kapellmeister at the early age of twenty-four. Precision and unanimity were the two qualities most admired in the band, and to this end Stamitz was probably one of the first leaders to take over from his harpsichordist the job of actually directing the orchestra. The training was so efficient that his successor, Cannabich, was able to control 'with a mere nod of his head and twitch of his elbow' an orchestra of almost fifty players — at that time the largest regular ensemble in Europe. Listening to the orchestra, said Schubart, 'one believed oneself to be transported to a magic island of sound. . . . No orchestra in the world ever equalled the Mannheimers' execution. Its *forte* is like thunder; its *crescendo* like a mighty waterfall; its *diminuendo* a gentle river disappearing into the distance; its *piano* is a breath of spring. The wind instruments could not be used to better advantage; they lift and carry, they reinforce and give life to the storm of the violins.'

There were, of course, some teething problems, and Burney pounced on his pet topic of intonation with schoolmasterly disapproval:

I found, however, an imperfection in this band common to all others that I have ever yet heard, but which I was in hopes would be removed by men so attentive and so able; the defect I mean is the want of truth in the wind instruments. I know it is natural to those instruments to be out of tune, but some of that art and diligence which these great performers have manifested in vanquishing difficulties of other kinds, would surely be well employed in correcting this leaven, which so much sours and corrupts all harmony. This was too plainly the case tonight, with the bassoons and hautbois, which were rather too sharp at the beginning, and continued growing sharper to the end of the opera.

To include a large wind section in an orchestra was both novel and daring; even the operatic scoring of the innovatory Rameau had scarcely used the wind section with such independence as did Stamitz in his largest symphonies. Wind instruments themselves had very recently undergone a rapid development, as a result of experimentation by so many of the instrument makers employed in European courts. The flute had been improved by the efforts of makers such as Philidor and the Hotteterre family, members of the French *Grande Ecurie*, or under the eagle eye of Frederick and the careful tuning techniques of Quantz in Berlin. The oboe, first made at the French court, was further developed there by

68. *The wind-band of Count Wallerstein (a gold silhouette, c.1785). The string bass was a usual addition to such ensembles.*

the Hotteterres, and Bohemia seemed to have a monopoly of virtuoso players on the natural horn — a result of the hunting-lodges maintained there by Hapsburg nobility with their bands of *cors de chasse*. Newest of all was the clarinet, an addition to the orchestra that intrigued Mozart the first time he heard it in Mannheim in 1777; 'Oh, if only we also had clarinets', he wrote when back at home in Salzburg; 'you cannot imagine the beautiful effect of a symphony with flutes, oboes and clarinets.' In fact Mozart's approval of the Mannheim wind players and the telling fact that he wrote a *sinfonia concertante* for the four best wind-players of the orchestra indicate that Burney's censure was unnecessarily harsh. It is difficult to believe that the oboist Ramm, who 'plays very well and has a delightfully pure tone', could have deserved the quartet and the concerto that Mozart wrote for him had his playing been as 'untruthful' as Burney suggests.

Another friend that Mozart made during his visit to Mannheim was Johann Baptist Wendling, one of the flute players of the orchestra. He introduced the young composer to a wealthy acquaintance of his, a flute-playing Dutchman from the East Indies (whom Mozart called 'my Indian'). It is thanks to 'my Indian's' commissions that we have the flute quartets and the flute concerto — though Mozart, at that time, professed very little enthusiasm for the sound of the flute. But it was neither the right time nor place to criticize; there was hardly a nobleman in Europe who did not attempt a few notes on the instrument, and the elector was no exception. Like Frederick, he was 'himself a very good performer on the German flute, and can, occasionally play his part upon the violoncello', Burney reported.

As the proficiency of their playing and the popularity of wind instruments increased, particularly under the second generation of Mannheim composers such as Richter, Fils, Cannabich and Holzbauer, so they became a separate department, independent of the full symphony orchestra. These wind bands, which might be as small as five players (two oboes, two horns and a bassoon) or as large as thirteen, were known as *Harmonie* and proved indispensible to the open-air serenade parties which were a part of summer life in the German courts. Moreover, for those who aspired to possessing their own orchestra, but could not muster the necessary capital, the solution of a resident wind band was most attractive. In an extremity it could easily be converted from cultural to military use. 'I heard music for wind instruments today, too, by Herr Mozart, in four movements — glorious and sublime,' enthused Johann Schinck. 'It consisted of thirteen instruments, viz. four horns, two oboes, two bassoons, two clarinets, two bassett horns, a double bass, and at each instrument sat a master — oh, what an effect it made — glorious and grand, excellent and sublime.' Like Samuel Pepys, Herr Schink was readily 'Ravish'd by the Winde Musicke'.

The end of this musical paradise came suddenly. On 30 December 1777, Maximilian III, Elector of Bavaria died. His heir Karl Theodore, who set out from Mannheim by moonlight on the first night of 1778, took with him his entire court, minus most of its musicians. Mozart and his mother were still there; she wrote, 'God grant that everything may turn out well, and that no troubles may come. I wish it with all my heart, for he is a very good ruler. Here now it is deadly quiet and thoroughly boring . . .' Silence reigned in Mannheim. The days were over when one could not cross the street without hearing a German flute, a bassoon or a clarinet. Musicians were pensioned off, the theatre stood empty, and the many aspirants to court posts had to turn elsewhere. Some tried Paris, some looked towards London — but for Mozart, and many others, there was only one possibility: Vienna.

TROIS TRIOS
Pour le Piano-Forte
Violon, et Violoncelle
Composés & Dediés
et Son Altesse Monseigneur le Prince
CHARLES de LICHNOWSKY
par
LOUIS van BEETHOVEN
Oeuvre 1.

'AUT CAESAR AUT NIHIL'

The courts of Europe did not expect to hear the individual voice of the musician raised to attract their attention. His product should be heard; if necessary he might be seen, after which he would be allowed the normal amenities of a servant, and then forgotten. Some establishments were more generous in their terms, and many individual patrons were considerably closer to their composers than to their cooks. Nevertheless, the same livery was worn by all. The most difficult thing for the nineteenth century to understand was that, in some cases, the composer was compliant and even proud of his position.

'Haydn was and remained an imperial lackey,' wrote Wagner, 'providing, as a musician, for the entertainment of his splendour-loving master. He was submissive and humble, and therefore the peace possible to a kindly, serene disposition remained with him till a ripe old age.' Given Wagner's unusual relationship with his patron, the mad Ludwig II of Bavaria, there is still very little understanding of a condition which many of Haydn's contemporaries would have envied. On the other hand, Haydn's own description of his situation is testimony to his shrewdness as well as his 'serene disposition'.

My prince was always satisfied with my works. Not only did I have the encouragement of constant approval, but as conductor of an orchestra I could make experiments, observe what produced an effect and what weakened it, and was thus in a position to improve, to alter, make additions or omissions, and be as bold as I pleased. I was cut off from the world; there was no one to confuse or torment me, and I was forced to become original.

It was a search for independence of mind rather than freedom of movement that occupied the composer during the latter half of the eighteenth century. The insistence on social equality, which eluded Mozart despite his public graces and came to Beethoven partly because of his lack of them, was of little interest to Haydn; he preferred to maintain his distance, and allow himself the right of comment. 'I have had converse with emperors, kings and a great many lords,' he told Griesinger in his old age, 'and have heard a great many flattering praises from them; but I do not wish to live on a familiar footing with such persons and prefer people of my own class.' From such a vantage point he could when in London note in his imperfect English: 'Milord Chatham, Minister of War, was so drunk for thrie days that he could not sign his name, with the rezult that his subawdinate, Lord Howe, togedder with the entire Fleet could not sale from London.'

It is not enough to accredit him with a naïve peasant sense of duty, nor a pathological fear of unemployment and starvation. Haydn was no revolutionary: while the Bastille was falling, he found no difficulty in attending to his duties specified by one of the most feudal contracts any composer can ever have signed.

Joseph Heyden will be considered an officer of the house. Therefore, His Serene Highness shows him the gracious trust that he will, as befits an honest house officer in a princely court, behave soberly and, to the musicians directed by him, not brutishly but gently, modestly, calmly and honestly, especially when music

69. *Haydn in 'romantic' pose at the square piano. (A coloured engraving based on the oil painting by Ludwig Guttenbrunn).*

is to be made in front of His Highness, and not only shall the Vice-Kapellmeister Joseph Heyden together with his subordinates, appear at all times clean and in livery, but he will also see that all those answering to him follow the instructions given to them and appear in white stockings, white shirt, powdered, and pig-tails, dressed alike.

Therefore

All musicians are subordinated to the Vice-Kapellmeister, consequently he will behave himself in an exemplary manner, so that his subordinates can follow the example of his good qualities; he will avoid any undue familiarity in eating and drinking or otherwise in his relations with them, lest he should lose the respect due to him, but will maintain his demeanour in such a way as to ensure that his subordinates obey him. Consequences that could arise from exaggerated familiarity should not lead to misunderstandings and quarrels.

At the command of His Serene Highness the Vice-Kapellmeister is liable to compose such music as His Serene Highness may require of him, such compositions are not to be communicated to any person, nor copied, but remain the property of His Serene Highness, and without the knowledge and permission of His Serene Highness, he is not to compose for any other person.

Joseph Heyden shall appear daily (whether in Vienna or on the estate) in the morning and in the afternoon in the ante-chamber and will be announced and will await the decision of His Serene Highness whether there should be music, and after having received the order will inform the other musicians, and not only appear himself punctually at the appointed time but also ensure that the rest appear, and should a musician either come late for the music or even be absent, he will take his name.

Should, regrettably, quarrels or complaints occur among the musicians, the Vice-Kapellmeister shall attempt in accordance with the circumstance to settle them, so that His Grace will not be importuned with trifling matters; but should a more important incident occur that he, Joseph Heyden, cannot himself settle by mediation, he shall faithfully report it to His Serene Highness.

The Vice-Kapellmeister shall survey and take care of all musical instruments, so that they should not be spoiled or made unusable through inattention or negligence.

Joseph Heyden is obliged to instruct the female singers, so that they should not forget in the country what they have learnt in Vienna from distinguished masters at great trouble and expense, and since the Vice-Kapellmeister has experience of various instruments, he will allow himself to be employed in playing all those instruments with which he is acquainted.

The Vice-Kapellmeister will receive herewith a copy of the convention and norms of behaviour of his subordinate musicians, so that he will know how to make them behave in service, in accordance with these regulations.

As it is not considered necessary to commit to paper all the services that he is obliged to perform, seeing that His Serene Highness graciously hopes that Joseph Heyden will in all matters spontaneously carry out not only the above-mentioned services, but also all other orders of His Grace that he may receive in future, and also maintain the music in good order so that he will become worthy of respect and of princely favour, all these shall be left to his skill and industry. In confidence of this

The Vice-Kapellmeister will be accorded by His Lordship four hundred gulden annually, payment to be made quarterly by the Chief Cashier. In addition to this Joseph Heyden shall receive his meals at the officers' table or half a gulden for board daily. Finally,

This convention was concluded on the 1st May 1761 with the Vice-Kapellmeister for at least three years, provided that if Joseph Heyden wishes to continue in this honour after having served for three years, he must announce his intention to His Lordship six months in advance, that is at the beginning of the third year. Similarly

His Lordship promises not only to keep Joseph Heyden in his service for the agreed period, but if he gives full satisfaction, he may expect the position of

70. *Haydn (seated in the foreground) at the end of a performance of* The Creation *in May 1808. This was his last public appearance. (Tradition holds that this scene shows him being congratulated by Beethoven).*

71. *Beethoven in 1823; a painting by Ferdinand Waldmüller.*

Principal Kapellmeister; should the contrary be the case however, His Serene Highness is free at any time to dismiss him from his service. Witness to which two identical copies have been prepared and exchanged. Vienna, 1 May 1761

Joseph Haydn

The immense gulf separating Haydn the court musician from Beethoven is immediately apparent from the draft contract that Beethoven drew up in order to alert possible patrons that he wished to occupy himself exclusively with the composition of large-scale works. He claimed that it must be the aspiration of every tone-poet (the term he preferred to 'composer') to free himself from the practical distractions of life.

1. Beethoven should receive from an exalted nobleman the assurance of a salary for life, even if several persons of high rank were to contribute to the sum fixed for this salary. This salary, in view of the present high cost of living, could not amount to less than 4,000 fl. per annum. Beethoven desires that the donors of this salary might then look upon themselves as having a share in the authorship of his new larger works, because they make it possible for him to devote himself to such works and relieve him of the need to attend to other duties.

2. Beethoven should always retain the liberty to travel in the interests of his art, because only on such travels can he become very well known and acquire some wealth for himself.

3. It would be his greatest desire and his most fervent wish one day to enter into the actual service of the Emperor and by means of the salary to be expected in such a position to be enabled to renounce the benefits set forth above either wholly or in part. Meanwhile even the title of Master of the Emperor's Music would make him very happy: should it be possible to obtain this title for him, his sojourn here would be even dearer to him.

Should this wish be fulfilled one day and should His Majesty grant him a salary, Beethoven will give up so much of the 4,000 fl. mentioned above as accrues to him from the Imperial salary; and should this salary even amount to 4,000 fl., he would then entirely renounce his claim upon the 4,000 fl. mentioned above.

4. As Beethoven also wishes to perform his new, larger works in the presence of a wider public, he requests an assurance from the Directorate of the Court Theatre and from their successors that on Palm Sunday every year the *Theater an der Wien* shall be placed at his disposal for a concert to be performed for his own benefit. In return, Beethoven would bind himself to devise and conduct a charity concert every year or, if unable to do so, to contribute a new work of his own to such a concert.

Surprisingly, the contract was accepted by the three aristocrats at whom it was aimed: the Archduke Rudolf, Beethoven's pupil in composition, put up 1,500 fl.,

72. *The Lobkowitz Palace in Vienna, where the 'Eroica' Symphony was first performed. (Painting by Bernardo Bellotto, nephew of Canaletto.)*

73. *Prince Ferdinand Kinsky, the dedicatee of Beethoven's C major Mass.*

Prince Lobkowitz 700 fl., and Prince Kinsky 1,800 fl. Their only rewards were the dedications prefacing Beethoven's compositions, always a sign of remuneration received or expected. But when Prince Kinsky was killed in a riding accident, Beethoven devoted a lengthy and far from obsequious correspondence in an attempt to rescue his annuity from the prince's representatives. Even Prince Lobkowitz had to be 'reminded' by the archduke, at Beethoven's insistence. 'All will go well', the composer wrote to a friend, 'the Archduke will take this Prince Fizlypuzly soundly by the ears . . .'

Despite relying on the aristocracy for finances, Beethoven never considered himself in their debt: 'nothing in the world is smaller than our great men', he wrote, '— yet I make an exception of Archdukes . . .' He had seen as much as he wanted of court life from the inside when, at the age of fourteen, he had been taken by Max Franz, the Elector of Cologne, to join his orchestra. He played both organ and viola there for two years, but, with the elector's generous help, was glad to leave for lessons with Haydn in that Mecca of all free-minded musicians of the late eighteenth century — Vienna.

The Austrian capital was a city of contradictions. One might look askance at the nobility of any town which could insert in the daily paper an advertisement: 'Wanted by nobleman, a servant who plays the violin well.' Yet the same city could boast an orchestra of princes and nobles that assembled to perform semi-private concerts to an audience of similar rank at the curious time of six in the morning! On the one hand the Empress herself could advise her son against employing the young Salzburger Mozart: 'What I say is do not burden yourself with useless persons and the claims of such persons on your service. It gives one's service a bad name when such people run about like beggars; he has, furthermore, a large family.' On the other hand, she could worship the composer Gluck, who first threw down the gauntlet of artistic immunity with the explicit conditions he demanded for the performance of his opera *Armide*: 'I must have at least two months in which to train my actors and actresses; and I must be at liberty to call as many rehearsals as I consider necessary; no part shall be doubled; another opera must be in readiness, in case any actor or actress shall fall sick. These are my conditions without which I shall keep *Armide* for my own pleasure . . . With it I think I shall close my career as an artist. The public, indeed will take as long to understand *Armide* as they did to understand *Alceste*.' And that was 1776, well before the French Revolution struck.

'Musicians are the only artists concerning whom the nobility display taste', claimed Riesbeck, several years before Beethoven arrived in the Austrian capital. 'Many houses maintain private bands for their own delectation, and all the public concerts prove that this field of art stands in high respect. It is possible to enlist four or five large orchestras here, all of them incomparable. The number of real

74. *A performance of Gluck's opera* Il Parnasso Confuso *at the Schönbrunn Palace in 1765. The cast consisted of members of the Imperial family, more of whom can be seen seated on the front row. The harpsichordist is presumably the composer.*

virtuosi is small, but as regards the orchestral musicians scarcely anything more beautiful is to be heard in the world.'

With a large empire to draw on, with the leading families of Hungary, Bohemia and Moravia all maintaining town as well as country palaces, with emigré musicians from 'the conservatoire of Europe' (as Burney called Bohemia) supplying an endless source of musical talent, with a musically educated bourgeoisie and a benign aristocracy, the conditions in and around Vienna fulfilled all the needs for the sudden flowering of the new instrumental music that made the Classical School of Haydn, Mozart and Beethoven.

Of this triumvirate Haydn was the one most protected from the dangers of the new era; life at the new palace of Esterházy, even though the prince had deliberately chosen a damp and windy swamp as his building site, was at least secure. Once building was completed, 'Nicholas the Magnificent' had a country seat to rival the King of France, at an expense of more than eleven million florins:

The castle is in Italian style, without visible roof, surrounded by a beautifully proportioned stone gallery. Most valuable are two rooms used by the prince. One of them contains ten Japanese panels in black lacquer adorned with golden flowers and landscapes, each of which cost more than a thousand florins. The chairs and divans are covered with golden fabric. There are also some extremely valuable cabinets and a bronze clock that plays the flute. In the second room, richly adorned with golden ornaments, is another gilded clock with a canary on top that moves and whistles pleasant tunes when the clock strikes, as well as an armchair that plays a flute solo when you sit on it. The chandeliers are made from

75. *The influence of Versailles; symmetry and splendour in the design of the palace of Esterházy.*

PROSPECT DER FÜRSTLICHEN   RESIDENZ ESZTERHAZ VON DEN
     HAUPT THOR   GEGEN NORDEN.

76. *Prince Nicholas Esterházy.*   77. *Baryton.*

artistically wrought rock crystal. In the library there are seventy-five hundred books, all exquisite editions, to which novelties are being added daily.

In an alley of wild chestnut trees stands the magnificent opera house. The boxes at the sides open into charming rooms furnished most luxuriously with fireplaces, divans, mirrors, and clocks. The theatre easily holds four hundred people. Every day, at 6, there is a performance of an Italian *opera seria* or *buffa* or of German comedy, always attended by the prince. Words cannot describe how both eye and ear are delighted here. When the music begins, its touching delicacy, the strength and force of the instruments penetrate the soul, for the great composer, Herr Haydn himself is conducting. But the audience is also overwhelmed by the admirable lighting and deceptively perfect stage settings. At first we see the clouds on which the gods are seated sink slowly to earth. Then the gods rise upward and instantly vanish, and then again everything is transformed into a delightful garden, an enchanted wood, or it may be, a glorious hall.

Opposite the opera house is the marionette theatre, built like a grotto. All the walls, niches, and apertures are covered with variegated stones, shells, and snails that afford a very curious and striking sight when they are illuminated. The theatre is rather large and the decorations are extremely artistic. The puppets are beautifully formed, and magnificently dressed; they play not only farces and comedies, but also *opera seria.* The performances in both theatres are open to everyone.

Behind the castle is the park. Everyone entering it stands still in amazement and admiration at the majestic sight, for it fills the soul with rapture. The park was built after the prince's own designs, and is without doubt the most gorgeous example of its kind in the whole kingdom. Art and nature are here combined in an extremely noble and magnificent way. In every corner there is something to attract the eye — statues, temples, grottoes, waterworks; everywhere are the glory of majesty, gentle smiles of nature, joy, and delight!

Even if it is true that this glowing description was actually written by Nicholas himself, the splendours of Esterházy were reiterated by every visitor in equally effusive terms. The prince's relations with his Kapellmeister were friendly but firm. Nicholas had a penchant for playing the *baryton*, a hybrid and complicated form of stringed instrument, with a sweet tone but little repertoire and Haydn was required to produce a continual sequence of trios for this instrument. If he failed, he would be firmly requested to 'apply himself to composition more diligently than heretofore'. Eventually Haydn wrote more than 160 *baryton* pieces for his patron, a repertoire of unfailing charm which he knew would never survive the obsolescence of the instrument. Nevertheless a command was a command — it is not hard to imagine what Beethoven's reply would have been!

With similar resilience, Haydn accommodated the deficiencies of the orchestra with only occasional and mild complaints about the rotten condition of the oboes, or the lack of violas. When the elector extended his residence in Esterházy, depriving the band of the holiday they had expected in Vienna, Haydn brought the point home to the prince with the greatest tact, in the 'Farewell' symphony. As the last movement neared its conclusion, each section of the orchestra in turn snuffed out the candles on their music-stands and left the concert hall, until only the front desk of violins remained in the growing gloom.

78. *An anonymous painting of Mozart at the age of six, in a costume given to him by the Empress Maria Theresa, for court wear. (It had originally been intended for the little Archduke Maximilian).*

When these finally took their leave, Nicholas relented and the court returned to the capital. The idea was whimsical, but the music was serious. This balance of opposites was peculiar to Haydn's character, and to the ambiguous position he was happy to accept — his lightheartedness, as Rossini pointed out, *was* his seriousness.

Compared to Haydn, Beethoven was a boor: the 'Grand Mogul' in the words of his great predecessor. The treatment he expected from others was rarely the treatment he himself gave. His contempt for the aristocracy was an ideal outlet for his bad manners; he shocked Goethe by telling him what happened when he had to give piano lessons to Duke Rainer:

He let me wait in the antechamber, and for that I gave his fingers a good twisting; when he asked me why I was so impatient I said that he had wasted my time in the anteroom and I could wait no longer with patience. After that he never let me wait again.

Even with the Archduke, whom he was inclined to except from his views on the upper classes, he could lose his temper. Mistakes in performance sent him into sudden rages: 'he would grow very red in the face while the veins on his temples and forehead began to swell; indeed, on one occasion he even bit his shoulder.'

One composer loved his employer, the other bit his patron on the shoulder — between these two extremes Mozart was the loser. With the frailty of genius, incapable of holding down a court job, dissatisfied with an assistant's position but temperamentally unsuited to life as a Kapellmeister, the young Mozart had trailed from city to city, ever hopeful but never succeeding. His position in Salzburg was abhorrent to him:

We lunch about twelve o'clock, unfortunately somewhat too early for me. Our party consists of two valets, the confectioner, the two cooks — and my insignificant self. By the way, the two valets sit at the top of the table, but at least I have the honour of being placed above the cooks. A good deal of coarse joking goes on, but no-one cracks jokes with me. . . . We do not meet for supper, but we each receive three ducats — which goes a long way! We had a concert yesterday at four o'clock . . . today we are to go to Prince Galitzin. If I get nothing, I shall go to the Archbishop and tell him with absolute frankness that if he will not allow me to earn anything, then he must pay me, for I cannot live at my own expense.

Archbishop Colloredo's reputation will probably never be rescued from the complexion given it in Mozart's letters — and it is no surprise to find that the recalcitrant composer was, both figuratively and literally, kicked out. We have already seen him in Mannheim, hoping for some position from the elector there. In Munich, the story was just the same:

When the Elector came up to me, I said: 'Your Highness will allow me to throw myself most humbly at your feet and offer you my services.' 'So you have left Salzburg for good?' 'Yes, your Highness, for good.' 'How is that? Have you had a row with him?' 'Not at all, your Highness. I only asked him for permission to travel, which he refused. So I was compelled to take this step, though indeed I had long been intending to clear out. For Salzburg is no place for me, I can assure you.' 'Good Heavens! There's a young man for you! But your father is still in Salzburg?' 'Yes, your Highness. He too throws himself most humbly at your feet, and so forth. I have been three times to Italy already, I have written three operas, I am a member of the Bologna Academy, where I had to past a test, at which many *maestri* have laboured and sweated for four or five hours, but which I finished in an hour. Let that be a proof that I am competent to serve at any court. My sole wish, however, is to serve your Highness, who himself is such a great —' 'Yes, my dear boy, but I have no vacancy. I am sorry. If only there were a vacancy.' 'I assure your Highness that I should not fail to do credit to Munich.' 'I know. But it is no good, for there is no vacancy here.' This he said as he walked away.

With neither the security of Esterházy, nor a pension from the Viennese aristocracy, Mozart was the only member of the triumvirate who relied entirely

79. Le thé à l'anglaise *at the residence of Prince Louis François de Conti. Very little attention appears to be directed towards the diminutive Mozart at the harpsichord. (Painting by Michel Barthélemy Ollivier).*

80. *Design for Mozart's* Magic Flute *by Josef and Peter Schaffer*, 1795.

on individual commissions and his own performances to earn an income. Even with his reputation as a child prodigy behind him, the reception he got could be far from warming:

I had to wait for half an hour in a large ice-cold, unheated room, which hadn't even a fireplace.

At last the Duchesse de Chabot appeared. She was very polite and asked me to make the best of the clavier in the room, as none of her own were in good condition. Would I perhaps try it? I said that I should be delighted to play something, but that it was impossible at the moment, as my fingers were numb with cold; and I asked her to have me taken at least to a room where there was a fire. 'Oh oui, Monsieur, vous avez raison' was all the reply I got. She then sat down and began to draw and continued to do so for a whole hour, having as company some gentlemen, who all sat in a circle round a big table, while I had the honour to wait. The windows and doors were open and not only my hands but my whole body and my feet were frozen and my head began to ache. There was *altum silentium* and I did not know what to do for cold, headache and boredom.

. . . At last, to cut my story short, I played on that miserable, wretched pianoforte. But what vexed me most of all was that Madame and all her gentlemen never interrupted their drawing for a moment, but went on intently, so that I had to play to the chairs, tables and walls. Under these detestable conditions I lost my patience. I therefore began to play the *Fischer Variations* and after playing half of them I stood up. Whereupon I received a shower of *eloges*. Upon which I said the only thing I had to say, which was, that I could not do myself justice on that clavier; and that I should very much like to fix some other day to play, when a better instrument would be available. But, as the Duchess would not hear of my going, I had to wait for another half-hour, until her husband came in. He sat down beside me and listened with the greatest attention and I — I forgot the cold and my headache and in spite of the wretched clavier, I played — as I played when I am in good spirits. Give me the best clavier in Europe with an audience who understand nothing, or don't want to understand and who do not feel with me in what I am playing, and I shall cease to feel any pleasure . . .

Even at the end of such ordeals, actual payment was often circumvented:

It was just as I had expected. No money, but a fine gold watch. At the moment ten carolins would have suited me better than the watch, which including the chains and the mottoes has been valued at twenty. What one needs on a journey is money; and let me tell you, I now have five watches. I am therefore seriously thinking of having an additional watch pocket on each leg of my trousers so that when I visit some great lord, I shall wear both watches (which, moreover, is now the 'mode'), so that it will not occur to him to present me with another one.

The blame for the failure of Mozart's career cannot be laid entirely at the door of the noble families. They had no experience (nor would they ever have) of dealing with an itinerant musician with the genius and temperament of Mozart. It was all very well to be dispatched round Europe by an ambitious father, with instructions to 'find your place among great people. *Aut Caesar aut nihil.*' There were already too many compliant Caesars, and no one wanted a querulous nothing. Mozart lacked the craftiness, as well as the tact, to break into the world, and, at least according to his father's diagnosis, he was both 'too patient or rather easy-going, too indolent, perhaps even too proud, in short, that he has the sum total of all those traits, which render a man inactive; on the other hand, he is too impatient, too hasty, and will not abide his time. Two opposing elements rule his nature, I mean, there is either too much or too little, never the golden mean. If he is not actually in want, then he is immediately satisfied and becomes indolent and lazy. If he has to bestir himself, then he realizes his worth and wants to make his fortune at once. Nothing must stand in his way; yet it is unfortunately the most capable people and those who possess outstanding genius who have the greatest obstacles to face.'

No one prevented Mozart from being buried in a pauper's grave with neither mourners nor gravestone. His 'Requiem', his last composition, was eventually sung for Haydn's funeral eighteen years later — the requiem also for a system of patronage nearing its end.

RETIRADA

The ivory tower is unimaginable as a feature of court architecture. Neither the turbulent fantasies of the Middle Ages nor the wildest follies of the baroque ran towards such an uncommunicative fastness. Only with the sudden blossoming in the nineteenth century of a speculative approach to culture could such a building be envisaged; and even then, it was an unattractive dwelling. Few artists outside the pages of poetry found it a desirable residence, and its first tenant, the poet Alfred de Vigny, seems to have been imprisoned only posthumously in his *tour d'ivoire* by his ill-natured biographer, Sainte-Beuve.

The liberated musician of the nineteenth century did not lack sources of patronage despite his defection from the court system; both public and publishers displayed voracious appetites. The dialogue between composer and performer that had traditionally taken place in the servants' quarters of the Waldstein and Esterházy palaces was now transferred to the music-houses of Artaria and Breitkopf. As elegant title-pages and neat engraving became an increasingly familiar sight in musical establishments, so the resident Kapellmeister was required less as a composer, and more as an efficient organizer and conductor. The composer, conversely, became disassociated from practical music-making, unless he could prove himself a virtuoso instrumentalist.

It is against this background of shifting obligations, rather than the isolationist philosophy of the ivory tower, that a nineteenth-century career in music should be judged. Beethoven succeeded as a performer with the public and as a composer with his publishers — partially by so obfuscating his contractual arrangements that they had very little idea what rights they could claim. By 1801 he could boast his independence:

My compositions bring in a good deal; and I may say that I am offered more

81. *The New Music Room of the Brighton Pavilion, with Christian Kramer in charge of the King's Household Band. On the left, George IV divides his attentions between Lady Conyngham and her daughter Elisabeth-Henrietta.*

commissions than it is possible for me to carry out. Moreover, for every composition I can count on six or seven publishers, or even more if I want them; people no longer come to an arrangement with me. I state my price and they pay.

Schubert, on the other hand, was a mediocre performer and an inefficient businessman. He was so uninterested in performing any music other than his own that he could not even qualify as a Kapellmeister; and he possessed a fault unpardonable in a courtier — he was notoriously unpunctual. It is one of the curious by-products of speculative romanticism that Schubert's disastrous bohemian career should have become the model 'life of the artist'. The garret, the wild excesses, the spontaneity of creation and the impoverished death are the legacy of Schubert not Mozart — indeed, contrary to the Romantic portrayal of Mozart's end, his income when he died was more than twice what his father had earned as a court employee.

Court patronage did not simply wilt and die at the first blast of liberation: its operations continued, although fewer composers thought it dignified to beat a path to the doors of their patrons. Some arrived as house guests, Brahms and Strauss, for example, in Saxe-Meiningen; others, like Chopin, were received 'into the first circles among ambassadors, princes and ministers'. On the other hand, there was the risk which Weber encountered in London, of being employed merely as an entertainer, without even the privilege of residence to compensate for the rudeness of the employer:

He performed, was paid, and then had to leave without being regarded as one of the guests of the house. The insolent lackeys served him differently from the 'guests', and would have blushed at the idea of offering him refreshments in the drawing room. His host greeted him condescendingly and pointed out to him his place, which, in many salons, was separated by a cord from that of the guests.

So much for the lionized Romantic genius.

   High-born amateurs sometimes intruded into these occasions. The Prince Regent's famous wind band, one of the costly attractions of the new Brighton Pavilion, sometimes found itself with 'Prinny' as its conductor, and Rossini, summoned for a musical evening, found he was expected to join the prince's light tenor in a duet or two. Even without royal participation, the prince's taste controlled the performances. Sir George Smart, after one particularly successful evening's entertainment, asked Kramer, the conductor of the band, how it was that all the tempi were so judiciously suited to the royal taste. 'Why,' said Kramer 'His Majesty always beats time to every movement: I watch him and beat the same time to the orchestra.' For such acquiescence, we learn that each member of the band was rewarded with 'supper, a pint of wine, and ale, in

82. *Ludwig II of Bavaria, by Gabriel Schachinger.*

83. *Richard Wagner (photogravure).*

addition to his pay'. The Prince Regent's expenditure, however, both on his music and his more amatory entertainment, was considered excessive and unproductive.

But to have maintained a full *kapelle* in the traditional style of court patronage would have been judged certainly quixotic and abnormal, probably mad. Ludwig of Bavaria had all these qualities. His grotesque patronage is redeemed for posterity in that it was directed at Wagner, and offered him the means of fulfilling his previously thwarted ideals of music–drama; the prolific opera critic Bernard Shaw pointed out that 'had Wagner been a Sandwich Islander he could have done nothing'. But the welcome that Ludwig offered him was hardly that of an objective connoisseur.

My only beloved Friend! My saviour! My god!
I rejoice in heavenly rapture, I am in ecstasy! Yesterday, when I read to Sophie your godlike letter announcing your coming, her cheeks glowed deep red, so heartily did she share my joy. Ah, *now* I am happy, now no longer abandoned disconsolate in the wilderness, for I know that my Only One draws near. Stay, oh stay! adored one for whom alone I live, with whom I die.

Your own

Ludwig

His excesses did not stop with personal relationships. According to Mark Twain (of all unexpected authorities), the demands he made of his theatre finally exploited to the full those elaborate devices included as safety measures by Frederick the Great's architect more than a century earlier:

In the enormous Opera House in Munich there is some sort of machinery which in case of fire can call an immense water power into play. This could, we are told, place the entire stage under water. On one occasion when the King was the sole audience a curious scene took place. In the piece a great storm is introduced; the theatre thunder rolled, the theatre wind blew, the noise of rain falling began. The King grew more and more excited; he was carried out of himself. He called from his box in a loud voice, 'Good, very good! Excellent! But I wish to have real rain! Turn on the water!'

The manager ventured to remonstrate: he spoke of the ruin to the decorations, the silk and velvet hangings, etc., but the King would not listen. 'Never mind, never mind! I wish to have real rain: turn on the cocks!' So it was done. The water deluged the stage, it streamed over the painted flowers and the painted hedges and the summer-houses; the singers in their fine costumes were wet from head to foot, but they tried to ignore the situation, and, being born and bred actors, succeeded. They sang on bravely. The King was in the seventh heaven; he clapped his hands and cried, 'Bravo! More thunder! More lightning! Make it rain harder! Let all the pipes loose! More! More! I will hang anyone who dares to put up an umbrella.'

To give the king his due, he is reported to have laughed heartily when shown that description.

84. *Brahms and Mühlfeld at Berchtesgaden on 30 September 1894, when they gave the first performance of the two clarinet sonatas.*

Wagner was unique in the extent to which he controlled his patron: the musician was now dictator, the king the petitioner. The judgement of posterity remembers Ludwig for making possible *The Ring* and Bayreuth, but his own people could not condone his profligacy and extravagance. Although he might happily have squandered his private fortune, public money was a different matter. But, even the removal of this once heroic figure, and the fall of the castle of Neuschwanstein — that Wagnerian transmogrification of the ivory tower — did not mark the end of music at court.

With all their traditional characteristics changed, and despite economic disasters, constant wars, and the reshaping of Europe by the Congress of Vienna, a few courts clung to their old principles of artistic support and pursued them into the present century. The court orchestra of the small principality of Saxe-Meiningen, with some forty-eight players, was the chief delight of its anachronistic, art-loving Duke Georg. Von Bülow, Richard Strauss and Reger all found employment there, the last appointment being terminated in 1913 at the death of the duke. It was there that Brahms, as a guest rather than an employee, first heard the clarinettist Mühlfeld. 'Nobody can blow the clarinet more beautifully than Herr Mühlfeld of this place', he wrote to Clara Schumann, and composed for him two sonatas, the clarinet trio and the clarinet quintet. The duke was magnanimous enough to tell Mühlfeld that if ever he wished to leave Meiningen to visit Brahms, he need not even ask permission.

85. *Costume design by Benois for Nijinsky's first appearance.*

86. *Costume design by Bakst for the ballet* Bouffon Russe.

Some courts further away from the centre of the storm survived even longer than Meiningen. The Imperial Orchestra and Theatre of St Petersburg, for instance, brought together the young Stravinsky and his first patron, Diaghilev; by a long stretch of the imagination it is possible to link works like the *Firebird*, and still later works such as *Oedipus* and *Les Noces* whose composition was supported by the Princess de Polignac, with the traditions of court patronage.

With the current patronage of the Shah of Persia, whose court composer produced, for the *son et lumière* festival of Persepolis, music only just within the capacious traditions of Versailles, or the compositions of the present King of Thailand, the theory of court patronage could be tenuously extended to the present day. But the essence of music at court is neither the setting, nor the resulting extravagance, but the relationship implied between patron and musician. Such an alliance of opposites rests on two important features that cannot be impersonated by any other system of patronage. One is the practicality of secure tenure that Bach commended in Dresden: 'Observe how the royal musicians are paid. They have no anxiety about their livelihood, and consequently are relieved of *chagrin*; each man is able to cultivate his own instrument and to make himself a competent and agreeable performer on it.' The other took its stand in the composer's psychology — his ability, or otherwise, to assume a pragmatic role in court life. It enabled the Duke of Ferrara to write to his secretary advising the appointment of Isaac in preference to Josquin, while admitting both to be incomparable artists. 'But', he stated with the objectivity of the true patron, 'Isaac is able to get on with his colleagues better and composes new pieces more quickly, while Josquin, although it is true he composes better, does so when it suits him, and not when one wishes him to.'

Mutual respect tempered with a wary misunderstanding has engendered many a masterpiece, and the wealth of peripheral anecdote should not deflect us from the implicit truth of Brahms's observation on royal immunity. Never criticize the choice of princes — the court has produced more music than the committee.

NOTES ON THE ILLUSTRATIONS

The publishers would like to thank the owners of the pictures listed below for their permission to reproduce them in this edition.

1. This painting from about 1450 decorates a wedding-chest, and depicts the marriage of Boccaccio Adimari and Lisa Ricasoli. The musicians are playing shawms and a slide-trumpet, typical accompaniment to a basse-danse. In the background is the baptistry of Florence Cathedral. *Accademia Florence: photo Scala.*

Title-page: A psaltery player from a fourteenth-century Italian miniature depicting Music and her attendants. *Biblioteca Nazionale, Naples: photo Scala.*

2. Miniature from a Flemish Book of Hours, *c.*1520. *Victoria and Albert Museum.*

INTRADA

Headpiece: Details from the title-page of *Syntagma Musicum* by Michael Praetorius (1620). *Mansell Collection.*

3. Several versions of this picture were produced by Mercier, or his studio, varying the background to show Kew House, Ham House or even a panelled interior. The violoncello that 'Poor Fred' is playing is without the endpin of a modern instrument. *National Portrait Gallery.*

4. According to the inscription, the première of *Alceste* was given 'à Versailles dans la cour de marbre du Chasteau éclaire depuis le haut jusqu'en bas d'une infinité de lumières'. *Mansell Collection.*

5. Court musicians at Florence. A. D. Gabbiani. Early eighteenth century. *Palazzo Pitti, Florence: photo Scala.*

6. The Bibiena family, collectively one of the greatest influences in baroque stage design, were responsible for much of the decoration and machinery of the opera at the Mannheim Court (see pp. 91ff). *Victoria and Albert Museum: photo Eileen Tweedy.*

7. Court of a Venetian Palace. Flemish School, *c.*1620. *Victoria and Albert Museum.*

8. 'The Triumph of Isabella.' 31 May 1615. Fifth in a series of six paintings by Denis van Alsloot. *Victoria and Albert Museum.*

CHAPTER I PRINCES OF HEAVEN AND EARTH

Headpiece: from *The Triumph of Maximilian* by Burgkmair, showing the emperor's organist Paul Hofhaimer playing the organ. Behind him is a regal, and (apparently) the outer case for the organ. 'By order of the Emperor' the inscription reads 'Hofhaimer artistically increased and enlightened music'. Vienna 1796. *British Museum: photo Eileen Tweedy.*

9. From Martin le Franc's poem *Le Champion des dames, c.*1440. *Bibliothèque Nationale, Paris: photo Giraudon.*

10. Court of King Yon of Gascony. *Bibliothèque d'Arsenal, Paris: photo Lauros-Giraudon.*

11. From *Le Chansonnier Cordiforme, c.*1470. *Bibliothèque Nationale, Paris: photo Bisonte.*

12. Court of King Philip the Good. *Musée de Versailles: photo Giraudon.*

13, 14. Two-thirds of a triptych by Hans Memling. *Musée d'Art, Anvers: photo Giraudon.*

15. Maximilian I. *Historisches Museum der Stadt, Wien: photo Österreichische Nationalbibliothek.*

16. Philip the Good, from the *Statutes of the Order of the Golden Fleece. Institut de Don Juan de Valencia, Madrid: photo Giraudon.*

17. Emperor Maximilian I and his family. *Accademia San Fernando, Madrid: photo Giraudon.*

18. Henry VIII's Musicians Gallery at Whitehall Palace. Drawing by Holbein. *British Museum: Fotomas Index.*

19. Illustration from Henry VIII's psalter. *British Library.*

CHAPTER II BRITANNIA TRIUMPHANS

Headpiece: A design for the proscenium of *Albion's Triumph* by Inigo Jones. Performed on 8 January

1632, this was the first production that Jones had undertaken after falling out with Ben Jonson; his collaborator here was Aurelian Townshend. *Trustees of the Chatsworth settlement.*

20. This virginals (surely one of the most over-decorated of all musical instruments) has been traditionally connected with Elizabeth, the daughter of James I. Although each of the eighteen panels depicting scenes from Ovid's *Metamorphoses* is worked in high relief in coloured glass, the association with the glass industry of Bohemia is unproven. The Winter Queen's connections were far stronger in the Low Countries than in Italy, and had she commissioned an instrument it would probably have been from Antwerp makers. However, the virginals may still have royal connections, since Paul Hentzner, travelling in England in 1598, noted 'a musical instrument made all of glass, except the strings' in the Hall at Hampton Court. *Victoria and Albert Museum: photo Eileen Tweedy.*

21. Queen Elizabeth playing the lute. Nicholas Hilliard. *Trustees of the late Lord Berkely.*

22. William Byrd, by N. Haym, 1719. *Mansell Collection.*

23. The quotation, for which I am indebted to Robert Spencer, comes from Dr. Plume's Library, Malden, Essex, pocket-book no. 25. The portrait, which has until quite recently been thought to represent the mother of Sir Philip Sidney (d.1586), can no longer be taken as evidence that the theorbo was known in England before Inigo Jones' return from Italy. *Viscount De L'Isle, VC, KG, Penshurst Place, Kent.*

24. Marguerite de Valois dancing *La Volta. Musée des Beaux-Arts, Rennes: photo Giraudon.*

25. Queen Elizabeth dancing *La Volta. Viscount De L'Isle, VC, KG, Penshurst Place, Kent.*

26. The wedding feast of Sir Henry Unton (detail). *National Portrait Gallery.*

27. The text of this very moving song has presented a problem to several generations of editors. In the last couplet of the first stanza Dowland has 'Com & posses my tired thoughts, worne soule,/That living dies . . .'. Several emendations have been offered, mostly preferring 'thought-worn soul' or similar variants. However, Dowland made no correction when the volume was reprinted; on the other hand, a slightly later setting of the poem by Robert Johnson *does* contain the words 'thought worne', so the score at the moment seems equal. A nicety of scholarship indeed! *British Library: Fotomas Index.*

28. Lucy Harington, Countess of Bedford, in Masque costume. John de Critz (attrib.). *Woburn Abbey Collection, the Marquess of Tavistock and Trustees of the Bedford Estates.*

29, 30. For more information on the Rosicrucian connections of the celebrations surrounding Elizabeth and Frederick, see *The Rosicrucian Enlightenment* by Frances Yates. Illustrations from *Der Beschreibung der Reiss. Victoria and Albert Museum Library: photo Eileen Tweedy.*

31. A nineteenth-century copy after a miniature by Simon van der Passe. *Victoria and Albert Museum.*

32. *Parthenia*, 1612-13. *British Library: Mansell Collection.*

CHAPTER III LE ROI SOLEIL

Headpiece: J. L. Berain: *Design for a male figure on horseback* and Henry Gissey: *Costume for a dancer. Victoria and Albert Museum: Michael Holford Library.*

33. Jean-Baptiste Lully. *Musée Condé, Chantilly: photo Giraudon.*

34. Louis XIV as 'Le Roi Soleil'. *Bibliothèque Nationale, Paris: photo Giraudon.*

35. Catherine de' Medici from the *Valois Tapestries. Uffizi, Florence: photo Scala.*

36. Country musicians: *Bibliothèque Nationale, Paris: photo Giraudon.*

37. Design by Torelli, 1678. *Österreichische Nationalbibliothek.*

38. Painting by Pierre-Denis Martin, 1722. *Château de Versailles: photo Lauros-Giraudon.*

39. Design by Berain for *Armide. Victoria and Albert Museum: photo Eileen Tweedy.*

40. Tableau of savages by Gissey. *Victoria and Albert Museum.*

41. Court Musicians by Puget 1688. *Musée du Louvre: photo Giraudon.*

42. Louis XIV and his family by Nocret. *Château de Versailles: photo C. F. L.-Giraudon.*

43. François Couperin le Grand. *Château de Versailles: photo Giraudon.*

CHAPTER IV ANNUS MIRABILIS

Headpiece: English eighteenth-century engraving of a concert performance. *British Museum: Mansell Collection.*

44. J. S. Bach by Haussmann, 1746. *Stadtgeschichtliches Museum, Leipzig: photo Bildarchiv Preussicher Kulturbesitz.*

45. Arcangelo Corelli, by Hugh Howard (attrib.). *Royal College of Music.*

46. Design by Juvarra for the Ottoboni theatre. *Victoria and Albert Museum.*

47. Handel by Dandridge (attrib.). *Syndics of the Fitzwilliam Museum, Cambridge.*

87. *Scene from the pageant retinue of Count Hohenlohe held at Stuttgart, 6 November 1609, to celebrate the marriage the previous day of Johann Friedrich, Duke of Württemberg to Barbara Sophia, daughter of the Elector of Brandenburg.*

Bibiena. *Royal Institute of British Architects, Drawings Collection.*

65. Maximilian III, Elector of Bavaria, by J. N. Grooth, 1758. *Schloss Nymphenburg: photo Mansell Collection.*

66. Karl Theodore, Elector of Bavaria, 1799. *Österreichische Nationalbibliothek.*

67. Outdoor concert at Schloss Ismaning by P. J. Horemans, *c.*1720. *Residenzmuseum, Munich: photo Joachim Blauel.*

68. Windband of Count Wallerstein. *Furstlich Oettingen-Wallerstein'sche Bibliothek und Kunstsammlung, Schloss Harburg.*

CHAPTER VII 'AUT CAESAR AUT NIHIL'

Headpiece: title-page of Beethoven's Op. 1 piano trios, published by Artaria, Vienna, 1795. *British Library: Fotomas Index.*

69. Haydn. Engraving after oil painting by Ludwig Guttenbrunn *c.*1791. *Victoria and Albert Museum, Enthoven Collection.*

70. Haydn at a performance of *The Creation*, 1808. *Bildarchiv Preussischer Kulturbesitz.*

71. Beethoven by Ferdinard Waldmüller, 1823. *Archiv für Kunst und Geschichte, Berlin.*

72. Lobkowitz Palace, Vienna, by Bernardo Bellotto. *Kunsthistorisches Museum, Vienna.*

73. Prince Ferdinard Kinsky, by Josef Kriehuber, 1812. *Österreichische Nationalbibliothek.*

74. Performance by the imperial family of *Il Parnasso Confuso* by Gluck. Painting by Johann Franz Grieppel. *Bundesdenkmalampt, Vienna.*

75. The Esterházy Palace by F. Landerer. *Bildarchiv Preussischer Kulturbesitz.*

76. Prince Nicholas Esterházy I. *Haydn Museum, Eisenstadt: photo Bildarchiv Preussischer Kulturbesitz.*

77. Baryton by Jacques Samprae, Berlin, *c.*1720. *Victoria and Albert Museum: photo Michael Holford Library.*

78. Mozart at the age of six. *Mozartmuseum, Salzburg: photo Scala.*

79. Mozart at the Conti court, by Michel Barthélemy Ollivier. *Musée du Louvre: photo Scala.*

80. Design for The Magic Flute by Josef and Peter Schaffer, 1795. *Mozartmuseum, Salzburg: photo Bisonte.*

RETIRADA

Headpiece: A water-colour caricature of David de Groot, solo clarinetist to King William I of Holland, by Alfred Edward Chalon. *British Library: Fotomas Index.*

81. The New Music Room at the Brighton Pavilion. *Royal Institute of British Architects.*

82. Ludwig II of Bavaria, by Gabriel Schachinger. *Bayerische Schlosser Verwaltung: photo Werner Neumeister.*

83. Wagner, photogravure by Hanfstaengl. *Theatre Museum, London.*

84. Brahms and Mühlfeld at Berchtesgaden, 1894. *Pamela Weston Collection.*

85. Costume design for Nijinsky by Benois. *Victoria and Albert Museum: photo Eileen Tweedy.*

86. Costume design for *Bouffon Russe* by Bakst. *Victoria and Albert Museum: Michael Holford Library* © *S.P.A.D.E.M.*

87. Pageant retinue of Count Hohenlohe, by G. Thonauer. *Victoria and Albert Museum: photo Eileen Tweedy.*

FOR FURTHER READING

Social histories of music are remarkably rare, and predictably partial. For a variety of English attitudes try Henry Raynor's *A Social History of Music* (Barrie & Jenkins), *English Chamber Music* by Ernst Meyer (Lawrence & Wishart), and *Musicians in English Society* by Walter L. Woodfill (Princeton University Press).

These divergences of interpretation are merely an extension, of course, of a similar bias to be found in original sources. It is well to remember Charles Burney's preference for everything Italian, and derision for the French manner when reading his *General History of Music* (to 1789) (reprinted by Dover Publications Inc., New York), or his accounts of the musical state of Europe in his own lifetime: *Dr. Burney's Musical Tours in Europe* (edited by Percy A. Scholes, Oxford University Press). Sir John Hawkins ('The Knight of the Freezing Quarto') gives a less eccentric account in *A General History of the Science and Practice of Music* (reprinted by Dover Publications Inc., New York) than Burney's sour epithet suggests. Both men published their rival histories in the same year, Hawkins anticipating Burney by a few months only!

The Amateur in Music, a compilation of quotations without over-interpretation, by F. H. Shera (Oxford University Press) places aristocratic patronage in perspective without developing too strong a conscience about the People's Music. J. A. Westrup gives a stronger exposition of historical principles in *An Introduction to Musical History* (Hutchinson's University Library) and the most readable proposition of the philosophical attitude is Gerald Abraham's *The Tradition of Western Music* (Oxford University Press).

Many of the most vivid views on court employment come from the musicians themselves; Mozart's letters to his family and friends (edited and translated by Emily Anderson — Macmillan), or a selection edited by Eric Blom (Penguin Books), are the most entertaining.

For the visual side of court entertainments, *Splendour at Court* by Roy Strong (Weidenfeld and Nicolson) offers a European cross-section, while from the same author *Festival Designs by Inigo Jones* (International Exhibition Foundation) and *The King's Arcadia* (Arts Council of Great Britain) offer well-annotated reproductions of designs for masque sets and costumes.

For some musical illustrations of the theme of this book, the reader is referred to a set of two long-playing records issued by The Folio Society containing instrumental and vocal music by Byrd, Rosseter, J. S. Bach, François Couperin, C. P. E. Bach, Frederick the Great and Mozart, performed by Christopher Hogwood and The Academy of Ancient Music.

Of the many friends who have offered invaluable advice and assistance, Heather Jarman, Judith Shackleton, Simon Shaw and Jan Smaczny deserve particular credit for innumerable improvements and felicitous touches.